SELF HELP & MENTAL HEALTH

Tough Path To Wellness (Our Story)

NICHOLAS LICAUSI

INKS&
BINDINGS

Inks and Bindings
888-290-5218
www.inksandbindings.com
orders@inksandbindings.com

Contents

Preface

This is a book I wrote with my dad since I had to live the path to wellness. This preface is like an abstract, which is a summary of a research study that allows readers to quickly learn about the important aspects of a study. In medical journals, an abstract is usually presented at the beginning of the published article. Abstracts are also a main vehicle of communication at scientific meetings.

This book will help everyone because there are supplements and biologics that this book talks about possibly reversing health conditions in your body that should be very helpful to everyone. My mom and dad worked their way through college and were very successful. My mom later got her bachelor's degree while working while I was in high school, and my dad got his aerospace engineering degree in college, and I got one year of engineering and I got one year of business at two universities.

I enjoyed being around my parents. My mom was also involved in our education, volunteering to help my teachers occasionally during my education. However, when I reached the age of twenty and was diagnosed with schizophrenia, my mom did not want me to live in with them in the same house.

Back then and even today there is a negative feeling about people that have a mental illness. Hopefully this will change because we are discovering new medicines that will put schizophrenia and other illnesses in remission.

People with schizophrenia can have their schizophrenia go into remission as long as I continue to take the prescribed medication and therapies. You can be taking pills every day or getting a shot as prescribed by a psychiatrist, which put your schizophrenia in remission. Sometimes when people get older, their mind can change in such a way that they may not need to take any medication. In my case, when I talk about schizophrenia being in remission, it is because I am taking the prescribed medication. Having schizophrenia in remission allows me to live in my own house and take care of things like a normal person. It also allows me to work and write this book.

A doctor would monitor a person and reduce the dosage if necessary or to see if they can take them off any medicine. The doctors don't have a process for taking people off psychiatric medication for schizophrenia except if you have problems with medicine. With other illnesses like T2D, if it goes away, they just take you off of it.

There are around fifteen million previously diagnosed patients that are really in remission, despite the statistics which should show that some of them should be but are not diagnosed as in remission of schizophrenia.

I was aware we correlated pot causing psychosis in some people. I was not aware when I was smoking pot and that this could lead to prodromal phase of schizophrenia. Prodromal is defined as process of changes or deterioration in the subjective or objectives that precede the onset of clinical psychotic symptoms. My parents were aware of me smoking pot and had me tested. Then they had us see a social worker and my parents told them I was using drugs and they recommended I go to a mental hospital. I went and got diagnosed with schizoaffective disorder paranoid type and atypical depression after being admitted.

This all became more difficult but it was probably the right thing to do in this case. My dad and I wrote this book to help others that have this illness, other illnesses, and also possibly help their families. The diagnoses of schizoaffective is very personal, and there's problems with that diagnosis with the depression, therefore, later the doctors change that to paranoid schizophrenia, which is in remission now, and my depression is in remission also.

Statistical analysis shows 36% of patients go into remission after six months to two years of therapeutic treatment in the United States, and it's a different percentage in every country. After five years, 58% of patients living in a therapeutic environment go into remission. However, despite these statistics, nobody is ever diagnosed as being in remission of schizophrenia or depression.

When someone is diagnosed with a mental illness, they are looked at differently by some people even if they are in remission. They have to be very careful how they act at all times.

Hopefully, this book will help everyone to learn how to treat someone with a mental illness and also help the person with the mental illness as well as others to adjust the way to talk with others about diseases and healthcare.

Also, one of the goals of the book is to give some ideas on what needs to be done so no one ever develops schizophrenia. Because once they do develop schizophrenia, they will be in some type of medication for the remainder of their life. Until we find a cure, we will also need to develop new medicines that will keep schizophrenia in remission. As I reviewed the initial draft of the book, one conclusion doctors should research is the effect of cannabis-induced psychosis and the effect it has on some people. A theory is that when the brain is being developed in certain people, they should not use drugs or it may lead to schizophrenia. It is best for no one to use drugs.

It is important to know as soon as you can to know what to do and catch it before it gets worse. That way they can get you off drugs and put you on medication and drugs and therapies like metabolic therapies which I will describe later in this book.

Also, psychosis is a short-term mental disorder involving a breakdown in the relation between thought, emotion, and behavior, leading to faulty perception, inappropriate actions and feelings, withdrawal from reality and personal relationships into fantasy and delusion, and a sense of mental fragmentation and separation from life.

You will see what happens to the family supporting the person with schizophrenia. It is very disillusioned to not know anything about this illness and to not make the lifestyle changes that are necessary.

The book will take you on a journey from first being diagnosed with schizophrenia, and problems encountered, and how I recovered through the years and about everyone's goals going forward. Hopefully, by reading this book, the person treated with schizophrenia and their family will be able to avoid the mistakes we made. Once you have made such mistakes, you know what they are and how to avoid them.

With support from the family and proper medication, if they diagnose people as in remission, then that person can still lead a normal life. It is the life you and your family wanted to live together before anyone got the illness.

The real challenge for the medical industry and government is to find a cure, so the person never gets long-term schizophrenia. We have a theory and a method for proving it described later in this book that will lead to a cure for schizophrenia. Until that happens, this book will give everyone an idea of what should be done to live a good life with this illness in remission. Also this book addresses the rights of the mentally ill and issues of biases of socio economic issues and unalienable rights that was promised in the 1948 United Nations declaration of human rights policy that was agreed upon by all nations but neglected and had no teeth and individual rights were altered by the different governments agendas and policies.

We need to make sure we do not give a stigma to the mentally ill.

I remember a psychologist telling me when I was in the first hospital we had to start the path to wellness and what to look forward to in my life. But because of this illness, it is apparent you still have possibilities and potential as you will see in the book.

This book can help you avoid some of the mistakes made and how you can lead a normal life if this ever happens to your family. The key is to get the proper medication and supplements from when you're in your fifteen to fifties. You can plan to change to the newer remedies or therapies for staying healthy for later in your life when there are more issues with your health as you get older.

The family needs to understand they will need to support the person with any condition and try to help them for the rest of their life. They also have to make plans to have the support for them after the family is not around to provide the support needed.

We told you why we are writing this book which is to help others with this illness and their families. I also thought back to when my father decided it would be a good idea to write the book. It was written a few years after I was let out of FEMA county jail and put on conditional release.

I thought it would be better with more education, so I studied metabolic syndrome and found 90% of everyone gets it sooner or later and put forth an outline of solutions to treating it yourself since doctors don't usually treat the root causes of mental health and diabetes. It is called psychophisiotherapy using the ketogenic diet.

After I had the opportunity to talk with the judge about my life with schizophrenia and diabetes and for my NGRI hearings the judge really understood I had been previously diagnosed and had been in treatment myself most of my life without getting in trouble before. I told her I never required rehospitalization after my initial phase and never committed and felony before

My family was very proud of me, so we thought it would be important for me to help others with this illness by writing this book. I am living with the illness in remission; I understand and know what it takes to stay out of trouble and stay healthy and live a good life.

It is also important for the family to understand the illness. When you read the book, you will see how family members could do better in supporting a person previously diagnosed with schizophrenia or the other diseases in remission.

Another important thing all people should do is to buy a Living Will Health Care Directive. You can do this by buying one from Legalzoom.com for $30 and completing this and also about buying your own medicines for yourself that will help you stay in charge and keep your rights.

By writing this book together, I learned much more about my life and hoped everyone learned more about this illness. It is difficult to write this book with my dad, but I believe this is the only way to write this type of book because these diseases affect the person who needs help with these illnesses and also may or may not require families working together depending on the situation with their families' supporting ability.

There were mistakes we both made along the way. As I said earlier, that is one of the reasons we wrote the book. We want the people reading the book to learn from our mistakes. Also, we make some suggestions at the end of the book, which, if implemented, may be able to eliminate schizophrenia or at least make it easier on the person with the illness and their families.

We have traveled around the world, and no matter where you go, homeless people live on the streets. Half of those people have some mental illness or are on drugs. We need to do something about that and hope we can make improvements by writing this book.

In the last chapter, we talk about a Medical Computer. This is something that does not exist today. We talk about what the computer will do and how it will change the medical industry and it can be within the scope of possibilities. We also discuss how the Medical Computer will help determine when diseases first get started and how it will help doctors and people worldwide. We also discuss supplements and other things that will complement the medication you are taking. Make sure you check any of these supplements and other things with your doctor to make sure they will be okay for you to take.

I also am trying online psychiatric evaluation, which is available now and would determine actual mental status and then the recommended therapies whether it is drugs or whatever. Usually if you're previously diagnosed and in remission, they would say you have no symptomology of psychiatric disorders and give you a drug therapy you can do at home. Also, online telepsychiatry is a lot less painful if you ever need to be yearly or seasonally reassessed and reevaluated, and they have medication management and psychotherapy and counseling, and that's even covered by insurance, so you can talk about how your new life is as it is now as an older patient.

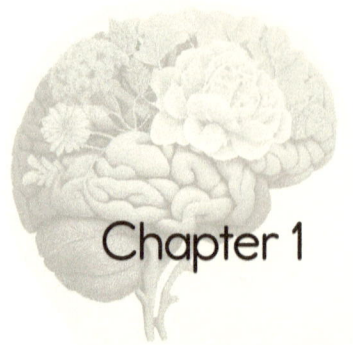

Chapter 1

When I First Noticed
I Had a Problem

I was in the prodromal phase of schizophrenia when I was in college and after and I had trouble with the education. I was passing some of my classes, but having trouble in others, and my family issues worsened.

Some people noticed I had been different after I got out of college, my parents didn't like that college didn't benefit my job situation. My dad told me I had to either join the military or go to a mental hospital so I went to the mental hospital. That had not changed after being diagnosed, and because they don't diagnose people as being in remission and being okay, I was labeled as being schizophrenic and mentally ill.

I had faced the reality that I was not failing school, but it was too hard, and I was not going to have the regular college degree I wanted. It was not a good economy, and there were few jobs I liked. There are a lot of problems created in college, and I was smoking a lot of pot. This could have been the main reason I became schizophrenic, or it could have been in my genes because there were people in my family that were schizophrenic.

My parents were not back from Japan yet, and the house we had was empty. I was living there, and my family hired someone to paint the inside so it would look nice when they returned.

I liked being at home again, but that was short lived soon after my parents returned from Japan. First, my sister, who started attending a local university, my mother, and then my dad returned; they all were different. We were all living at home, but it wasn't the same. We got our furniture and house-related expenses taken care of, but we had created more problems from being apart too long, and once parted, it was hard to come back to the way we were.

Before my parents returned, the neighborhood friends had been over a lot. My old friends came over a lot before they came back, but I had to stop hanging out when my parents came back from Japan, and there was a drug issue with pot.

My parents decided it would be good for me to go to the university my mom graduated from and my sister was attending.

I tried doing it, but that was when my parents and I knew something was wrong with the schools after high school, they were a lot harder after I became ill. My father took me to a psychologist, and she recommended my parents put me in a mental hospital. This was based on a drug test my dad had made me get to get me help.

After the time I had schizoaffective disorder I had to live separated from my parents since my mom and dad felt about it. This created this separation with my family.

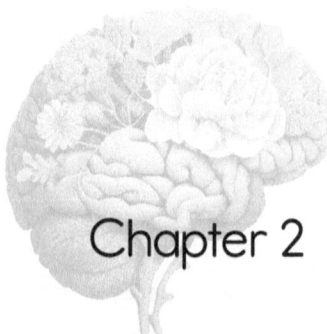

Chapter 2

When My Family First Noticed I Had a Problem

Later in the book, we will talk about a proposed way to determine how people become schizophrenic. There is some proof that pot can make some people psychotic and that leads to schizophrenia. We need to gather data on what people were doing before they became schizophrenic. From that data, we will be able to see a pattern and then determine how people become schizophrenic.

Now I have read that pot may cause psychosis, but one cause of psychosis is schizophrenia also. If they knew for sure it did, then I would believe there would be a big announcement that a drug-induced psychosis is permanent. That is one of the reasons we believe there should be a Medical Computer and data gathered by online telepsychiatry or other methods of gathering this data.

We never even thought about schizophrenia or other diseases when we got back from Japan. We had just gotten back after spending three years in Japan, so we were surprised by the way our son was acting.

We first thought we should practice tough love with him. This did not work with our son. We knew our son would not hurt us, but we could not figure out why he was acting very different.

We finally decided to get a blood test for pot and see a psychologist, but we were not thinking about schizophrenia at that time, just the marijuana abuse. Then we had me drug-tested for marijuana use and the test showed the marijuana use. Then my dad had us see a social worker together, and he informed her I had used marijuana, and I was tested then she suggested we put him in a hospital because of substance abuse and find out for sure if our son had schizophrenia.

That is something I would suggest to anyone with a person that is acting very different from how they used to act and you cannot figure out why. Rather than seeing a psychologist, I would suggest they see a psychiatrist first before checking in to a mental hospital. We were treating him bad because we were not sure what to do.

They believe environmental issues, genes, being at a low point, and drug addiction is what causes this illness. We understand healthcare, but families must understand they have to help support people diagnosed with schizophrenia more than they have ever done before.

My parents should have put less pressure on me because they were hoping I could still achieve my original goals. My parents should have helped me more in adjusting my goals and put less pressure on me. You can see they separated us further apart because they were not educated on schizophrenia and the stigma that is attached to schizophrenia even today. A person with schizophrenia and has been labeled with that illness has to be very careful how they act. If you raise your voice or try to argue a point, it can make people very nervous if you have a schizophrenia label. So rather than argue a point even if you are right, it may be best to not argue a point.

When we are diagnosed with schizophrenia, we know it is a preexisting non-life-threatening lifetime diagnosis, but they should start diagnosing people in remission of schizophrenia and depression even if they are out of the FEMA county system living in the community with their parents or by themselves.

At the first hospital, they had a program set up where my parents would go to group sessions, and we would discuss the treatment plans and getting out, but we know the situation was not as good as before getting diagnosed. When I was first diagnosed and in the first hospital, we asked my godfather Paul to come to the hospital and check in on us. He had said I had ups and downs and that seemed true, but I wasn't very up at the time. That hospital wanted my parents to come to daily meetings and asked that we stay there for a while. My father got me a personal computer the first one was an IBM PS2, but we did not have the internet yet. It was a very hard time for me despite having a computer and a little car when I first got this diagnosis.

At the first hospital, my father proposed to the hospital the Medical Computer we have described in this book. He said he would work on it with their team, but they declined. If they would have adopted the proposal, then by this time we would have found a cure for schizophrenia and many other diseases and eliminated a lot of suffering. The Medical Computer described in the book and The Medical Project by Nicholas Licausi if built back then would also have stopped the spread of Covid. Concerning the insurance I have, I don't want to change my original Medicare to an advantage PPO plan right now. This is because of medicare advantage healthcare plan insurance takeovers in forensics cases. It's healthcare fraud with government papers they can fill out with social workers or doctors and others who can and then try to fill out that paperwork and become your main provider on the PPO plan and then they can send you away. Knowing this beforehand helped, and because I have original Medicare and not an insurance PPO company, I'm still here right now. They try but many can be very cheap with helping yourself sometimes it's just good food or supplements, but I help myself so there's no big bill for insurance. I won't have this insurance issue in two months by getting a lawyer after the case is closed, and then after it is terminated, it might be okay to switch, but just in case I need surgery or something and I don't need it before we close the case in two months and it's terminated, then maybe I'll reconsider this issue but definitely not right now. Once the Medical Computer as described later in the book is built, people will be able to practice more self-help. You would think this would be something the government would take on with all the engineers, programmers, and money they have. If not the government, then maybe a large company, hospital, or software firm might take on healthcare for its employees and families and charge it off to health insurance costs or divert that money into corporate healthcare supplements.

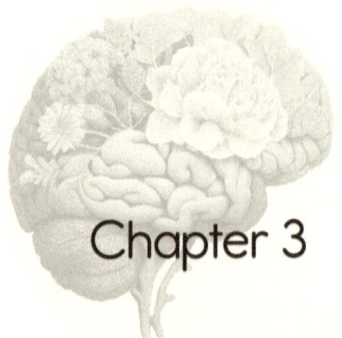

Chapter 3

Years of Doctors, Hospitals, and Schools

The Patient

Research suggests a combination of physical, genetic, psychological, and environmental factors can make a person more likely to develop schizophrenia. Some people may get in the prodromal phase of scitzophrenia from using drugs or pot combined with an overemotional or stressful life that may trigger their loved ones to get them help. Its good to see a psychiatrist if that happens and not just check yourself into a mental hospital yourselves or have someone else do it. But regular psychiatrist were rarely ever been able to undiagnosed a patient once their diagnosed and it requires a lot of work to diagnose a patient in remission and probably would need the medical computer and a good doctor. As I said earlier the first time, I was diagnosed with schizophrenia in remission was in FEMA county jail system, which was around forty years after I was first diagnosed schizophrenic.

I learned to handle being schizophrenic in today's society. I have to be very careful how I act all the time with this preexisting condition which was non-life threatening.

I had to decide to go to college again. I took aircraft mechanics in Daytona Beach. My parents were doing everything they could to support me in paying for all my college, apartment, and food.

I also got to take flying lessons to get my pilot's license and got a solo license. I also got into aircraft mechanics at college, but after going to that school, I found I was not into going into the profession of aircraft mechanics, so I left school and went back home to Ft. Lauderdale and got an apartment. I switched apartment complexes, and my dad got mad about that and said I had to go to a mental hospital or my grandmother's, so I chose to live with my grandmother.

There were two uncles that did not want me there, but my grandmother wanted me to stay with her. After a while, my uncle had called some social workers who talked to my family, and they took me out of my grandmother's house and put me in a mental hospital in Miami.

That hospital was pretty bad; they said the medicine I was taking wasn't any good and they put me on Haldol and Thorazine. I later got out of the hospital after eleven months of hell and went to a treatment center in Miami. After three months, I wanted to go to a better treatment center in Orlando that my parents and I found out about while at the first hospital.

An ambulance drove me to the residential treatment center in Orange County, and I remember driving into Winter Park, and it looked cool. I was finally in a good place. I got a treatment plan and saw my third doctor there. I still never smoked pot or cigarettes but had some mental health issues I had to work out, and I did it.

I found out they had an apartment program in Fern Park, which was a part of the same residential treatment program I was in and I was able to go there. I also could get that paid for with insurance for the first year and a half, and then later I found an apartment program that I could pay for myself, so I got into the apartment program.

After a while, I was told by my doctor I had to get a trade job, and we found a job at a furniture shop. My parents were still paying for some of my living expenses, but we had an overpayment from my SSI from saving up over $2,000 in social security, which they saw in my bank account. Social security had to set up a repayment plan for me to pay back what I got for three years and still got my social security. However, social security had to cancel that debt when I got SSDI later on under my dad.

I got a little sick after a few months living on my own, I think it was a slight case of ischemia hyper fusion from low pH and low oxygenation in my blood. Celiacs disease is related to ischemia, which is from low pH and low oxygen, I think these diseases are also related to sleep apnea. I think I had slight cases of all three illnesses before I learned how to fix them with alkaline water and supplements. I later called my old counselor, and he hooked me up with my old friends who were living in the apartment program. We paid for it together by working and also my getting social security and my parents. I later moved to another friend's house. At that time, I had my 1981 Camaro with was all hail damaged by a storm. It got me around but was hail damaged from a storm and I traded it in for a four-wheeler truck.

Then my old counselor from the apartment program found me another apartment in that program, and I had to trade back in my truck and get my apartment in the aftercare program officially again with my old counselor. We were able to get it, and all that paid for again with the counselor and my mom in the aftercare apartment program. I was still seeing the same psychiatrist I was seeing before from the residential treatment center I was in.

While I was living in the apartment program, I dropped a glass on my finger and cut it really bad and I had to get microsurgery. After the surgery, I had therapy for my hand. I was lucky I can still use my hand and bend my finger all the way. My low alkaline and low oxygen in my blood got better from the drugs naproxen I got during the surgery, but my cut looked very green and ugly before it healed. After a few years of seeing my psychiatrist in the aftercare program, while I was there, the treatment center offered a cruise trip to Cozumel, so everyone from the treatment center went on a cruise. It was fun, but when I got back, I found out the apartment program I was in was going under new management. My counselors that ran the program were leaving, and I could not keep my deals for that lower price with the new counselors I just met recently. Then 9-11 happened. It was shocking, and we couldn't talk about it that much. My new counselors all watched it while we went to groups, and a few weeks later, my rent went way up, so I wanted to leave to have my own place just as cheap. It was cheaper that way and my parents would support me again and I wouldn't have groups. I still had been seeing the psychiatrist I had switched to before.

My father willingly came to help, and we quickly found an apartment I could live in. It was a one-bedroom. We found the first one-bedroom in Altamonte Springs and then another three one-bedrooms in Sanford in the same place. It was a big three-story apartment complex, and I stayed there for four years, and I switched to three different apartments there. I started back doing my old hobby of building and flying model planes; during that time, my parents came up to see me twice and to see my apartments and go out to eat. I was in the clubs and flew in a model airplane contest and also did RC cars. I was not able to win a trophy, but I was in the two clubs in Sanford. I had made a few flying buddies in the clubs, and I flew fun fly sport planes; I was pretty good at flying since I did it all before.

I did spend a lot of time at the local hobby shops and was still into computers and I bought and built PCs. I had seen my psychiatrist for a long time by then, and we had advanced psychotherapy for many years. I talked about everything I was doing, and my psychotherapy lasted for twenty-five years with him, but it was not good for diagnosing people like myself in remission, but he should have said it or I should have asked if I was. Furthermore, I was functioning independently and had my own house and very productive and was making money and had a sense of empowerment and overcame negative feelings and stigma and didn't get any great news from him, just a pat on my back every once in a while.

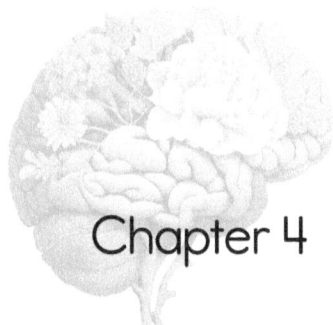

Chapter 4

My First House

The Family

My dad is an aerospace engineer, so you think he would believe in real space vehicles if there were any, but he did not. Some people in the secret government that do can even lose their jobs by talking about this.

We found my first house in Deltona, which is close to Orlando; the house looked nice, but there was something I didn't know when we bought it. I saw extraterrestrials living behind our house and saw lights at night and later found there were two real aerial phenomena ships, one big and one small. I remember seeing a red light in the woods that later turned out to be the rear thruster of a real classified unidentified flying object (UFO), the big one. I filmed them flying in formation in the night sky with a super 8 polaroid camcorder. I made it into a movie I still have today. There were cops driving by ignoring it and people shooting guns at them from across the street, and my cameras were rolling a lot from my bedroom window of the lights in the sky and my drone videos. I was seen by several types of extraterrestrials who later left when the government knew. Finally, the government shook them out when the city took out their spot in woods on the back and side of my house when the city widened the road near where they were and took out the trees and put in retention ponds for the new sewer system they put in.

I was still seeing my psychiatrist and told him about it being near my house, but he didn't care. He retired eight years later, saying I should see another doctor and talk about moving out of that house. When I told my parents, they said maybe in the future, but they didn't want to move. Nevertheless, we had the house all fixed up to sell.

The next thing that happened got me into a lot of trouble. There was a post in the back of the house in the parking area. It looked like an electromagnetic device on the post which my backyard neighbor put there. I was worried it would harm me, so I went and disconnected it. I put it in my sink and put water over it and it popped. It looked like it was very high-tech military. I later left a picture of the device when it was there with message and sent the photo to the police to tell them what my neighbor did. I was already shaken up quite a bit, and I was a little too edgy and I wanted to get my neighbor in trouble for what he was doing with the device on his pole in his yard. I wasn't thinking that I could have been put in jail for a felony for years if I told on him. The police had the photos, and they knew I gave it to them. They didn't see the real device on that pole on my neighbor's yard because I already removed the device from that pole. There is what's called for reporting suspicious devices the 4Ws shown on the Department of Homeland Security when you do that: (1) Who or what it is? (2) When did it occur? (3) Where did it occur? (4) Why did it look suspicious?

Apparently, I left out when it occurred which was three days prior. Also, I never reported the UFOs. I should have left sooner, but I tried everything I could with my parents. I think my parents did not believe I really saw something; they did not know what the psychiatrist said, and they did not want to go through the aggravation of buying and selling the house. I don't know what I would do if I couldn't put a cattle magnet on my head every once in a while if I get shocked to dissipate the electric shock.

The police came to my house and saw me and wanted to arrest me. I resisted arrest, and I went back inside my house and drew a bath and I put my head under the water and put on my new gas mask and I had hazmat suits too. Since I did not come out, they shot tear gas into the windows of my house and later used robots called molly to break down the front door and the bedroom door and bathroom door with little explosives and they then pulled me out of my house.

Since the post was on my neighbor's property and there was no bomb on the post when they looked, they put me in jail for calling in two false reports for the same thing. I got two charges for it because when the device was on the post because I called the police two times.

I discussed how it happened with the corrections officers when I was in jail and I told them about the device and how I removed it already before the police got there. They knew one count was a mistake and the second charge they couldn't remove because they classified the report I gave to them and they only removed one of the counts then I still had one count left and I got an NGRI for that.

The judge found me not guilty by reason of insanity (NGRI) because the public defender didn't want to describe the whole story and go for the not guilty plea, so they decided we go for the not guilty by reason of insanity plea after eight months in jail.

After being released from jail, I was living in the community but with supervision for two years. I had to do a lot of community service type work and had to go to church since it was faith-based. I started smoking cigarettes at the place because they all did it. I had to quit later, but it was hard. I used nicotine lozenges for two years. Later I had to go to an assisted living program for two years. My parents sold the house while I was in jail since the police did too much damage and we didn't have the house secured to be empty without me living there to take care of it. I left my car and all my stuff at the house. I couldn't have my car back for two years. I also needed to get my mental health medicine, get blood work done, reverse my insulin resistance type two diabetes (T2D), high blood pressure, and cholesterol. I was able to lower all my blood marker levels and got them way down since then.

I had some medication for all three problems I had in jail, which I later got better medicine. I did more research and then would buy myself supplements. I still have a healthcare directive living will on the cloud computer which I kept with all my other stuff.

After the two years were done there, I got to leave the program. I had to get that approved by the judge first and my case manager, but then I got my own apartment with public housing choice voucher to save money and afford to pay myself. I still didn't get full support system from my parents back yet, but after one more year, I did get back my family support system I had before.

We decided to modify my conditional release again and leave the apartment in Daytona after about a year because it was very small and in a bad area, and public housing wasn't that great, and my family bought me my second house. We thought if I got our own house, it would be a lot better investment and I would not have to deal with public housing vouchers, and it is better for me to get off conditional release and work on my own things.

I have a modified conditional release plan, which was part of what you need to modify again when you can get a house in the community and on unconditional release. I had to fill my apartment with new stuff using money I had saved for while I was in jail; I saved up almost $17,000 because I didn't have to spend anything while it was NGRI until I got out, but I was still saving a lot of money.

I bought nice furniture for the house from the apartment and a washer and dryer and other food and stuff from my apartment, which I moved to the house. The house is nice, it's a lot older than the first house, and we bought it with money made from selling the first house.

Since moving into the house, I am finding that the easiest but not the cheapest way to live is to go shopping online. I started eating delivered meat with a ketovore diet and really am reversing insulin resistance diabetes and lowering cholesterol. I used to eat carbohydrates and non-GMO, but that's bad for the diabetes. I also know about fixing the root causes of the diabetes which is the insulin resistance.

After eating the GMO food in jail and right after I got out of jail, I have put on a few pounds, so I developed another hobby. I am focused on nutrition and made it part of my healthcare directives and I keep buying and taking all my supplements I found by researching all the new supplements which will help eliminate the illnesses I have. I used to buy a lot of food supplements and biologics before, but now I researched more about all my diseases I got diagnosed for during the time I was on conditional release the last four years, and there was a lot of improvements in treating diseases yourself with supplements you can buy yourself and eating right. I do this with the help of my doctors.

I watched many healthcare doctors on YouTube to find out all this over the last four years while I was on Metformin and I changed that to AMPK activators and Nrf2 activators and other stuff that I will mention later and I hardly eat any carbs or sugar. I take over-the-counter supplements for preventative cancer, anti-aging, cardiovascular, high blood pressure, and my insulin resistance type two diabetes before, but now they are selling better supplements online.

Some people don't like to work harder when they are dying, but that's what it's like, and it depends on if you want to succumb to death or not, but that's up to each individual. When you are buying supplements or something, watch out for redundancies because you don't want to take another nutrient or another supplement or vital nutrient if you already have in one you are taking.

I was focused on keeping diabetes in check. I wanted to lose some weight and fix my insulin resistance. Over the last four years, my HBA1C went from to 6.7 to 6.4, and it went up to 6.6 right now almost the same as it was before. I might get it to go lower soon because I treat it better now and cut out a lot of carbs. I am also fixing my insulin resistance better by eating a ketovore diet. I will talk about all of my generally accepted healthcare standard medicine and supplements.

I have always been concerned about my health so earlier in 2016, I put together an advanced healthcare directive living will. It makes known my desire that my life be artificially prolonged as long as reasonably possible within the limits of generally accepted healthcare standards.

I hope I can get off of conditional release soon because I am doing everything I am supposed to do while on conditional release. I am following the prescribed healthcare directive given me, I have a living will and I have good standing in the community and insights into mental health and substance abuse.

I also have strong ties to the community, and I have a house and I am in control of my health. You can plan ahead and do things during various times of your life to prepare, and you can take supplements when you want to keep ahead of the dying problem and stay healthy. Also you can refrain from smoking pot the wrong ways. If needed, you can use a doctor to smoke medical marijuana instead of doing it wrong way which is what started this problem with schizophrenia.

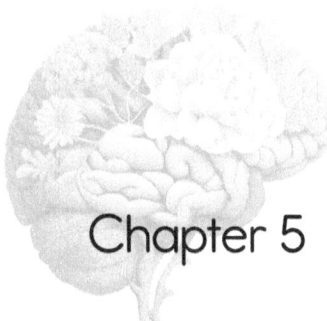

Chapter 5

Family Helped with Doctors, Appointments, and Hospitals

The Family

I say a prayer every day for my son to have health and happiness. He also prays to be healed. He later found cures for his body and has done it himself with the help of doctors. He will explain how you can do it yourself later, which is the key to fixing all that was done in error.

When my son was in the first hospital, I took extra-long lunch breaks from work and put in extra hours so I could see him and his doctors at the mental hospital. One thing we learned is that schizophrenia can hit every family and changes everything that family does.

At the time he was diagnosed in 1987, it was assumed that a person first diagnosed with schizophrenia would be in and out of the hospital, apartments, and maybe jail since they are not diagnosed in remission. I remember asking Paul, a friend who was best man at my wedding and became a psychiatrist, when my son was born, since my brother was schizophrenic, about schizophrenia since it ran in my family and him telling me not to worry because he thought there would be a cure by the time my son became a teenager.

Today there still is very little understanding of how someone gets schizophrenia, except for some studies showing pot may cause psychosis which could lead to schizophrenia. That is why I think more work needs to be done. This disease is really hard on some families. My family and I had really good insurance, and after several months, they decided it was okay for him to leave the hospital. After the first hospital, we really did not have a good plan for what to do next except to get an apartment for him which we did in south Florida.

The insurance program dictates how long a person can stay in the hospital, or you need to be very rich to keep them in longer. After a certain period, the insurance makes you pay for some of the hospital cost. The insurance usually does not cover you after you get out of the hospital. Since my mother had a hard time dealing with this illness, my father could not do anything to help me stay with my family. My family and I paid for some of the costs that occurred during my whole life.

We were lucky to find a long care treatment center place in Orlando and for me to go there after I had to separate with my family but what is needed is a better plan that can be followed by families that had children with similar circumstances who need their families support system and the same healthcare directives as their families. When I was under a doctor's care, it gave me someone to talk to when my father was busy.

When I look back at what was happening, I wish they could have listened more to what I was trying to tell them.

We will discuss the best options a doctor can take for people with schizophrenia in remission. The hospitals I have stayed at have a difficult time diagnosing schizophrenia and also when it is in remission. The problem we have today is that there is no suggestion of what to do to get diagnosed as in remission. The only time I was told my schizophrenia was in remission was when I was released from county FEMA jail system.

We were lucky to find a place in Orlando when I was first diagnosed with schizophrenia. What is needed is is for families to follow up with their children not kick them out whether they have schizophrenia or not and they need their own health care directives and their support systems.

This would not be easy to implement. In some cases, it would be nice to outline how parents should take care of their sons or daughters. This would allow the person to live a normal life with their family in their family's house with the support of their parents.

This is why mental health patients as well as doctors could and should have a lot of insight into mental illness and substance abuse to share with parents. This is not done today, and it should have been done when I was in the first hospital.

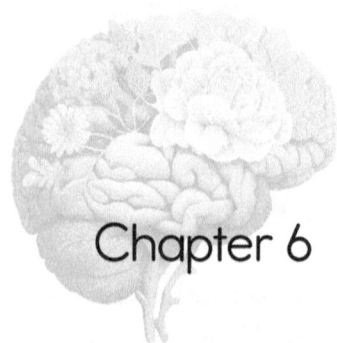

Chapter 6

Even today with all my son's problems gone away, we are so proud of how he handled everything

My father was doing well at work, and he got an opportunity of a lifetime to take an assignment in Japan with a promotion and more money. It was something that would help the whole world. The company my father was with would pay for a private school in Japan for my sister and I would stay at college. They would pay for two trips a year from college with stopovers in California or Hawaii and for me to be with the family in Tokyo until college started up again.

I was in my second year of college, and my sister was a senior at The American School in Japan.

While on assignment in Japan, the company my dad was with also paid for an around-the-world trip for our whole family. We stopped in all the big cities, but I remember two of them well. One of the stops was in London, then we went to Paris, then we drove to Switzerland in a rental car and went skiing in the Swiss alps.

Anyway, the trip around the world was one of the best trips ever. Sad to say, it was our last trip together, but it was a happy memory, and we will never forget the fun we had together.

I will always love my parents whether they are here on earth with me or in heaven. I pray for them every day. I am really happy that I agreed to write this book because we are both learning more about each other and also how to help people with schizophrenia and other diseases.

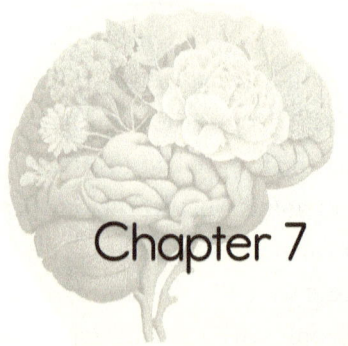

Chapter 7

Family's View of What Happened at First House

Patient and Family

One of the problems I had with the first house was the water coming in from the city, so we installed a whole house water filter system to purify the water. Those don't filter out acid, and you really need an alkaline water pH water filter pitcher for putting antioxidant effects in water.

After living in the house for a couple of years, I had a problem with the police. There was a communication problem between the police and myself. They said I made two false reports and I was trying to report a previously removed electromagnetic device that was behind my house. I thought I was doing the right thing by reporting an electromagnetic device, and I am not sure what the police thought about them not seeing it after I told them it was removed already. The Department of Homeland Security says you should report anything suspicious to the police and that some of the reports may be mistakes, but we should report them anyway. The Department of Homeland Security should put a warning label that says if it is not a harmful device after the police come out to see it and they don't see it right, then you will be arrested. If I did report it or not and it was or was not a harmful device, then I should not have gotten arrested because of my story of what happened.

I did send my dad an email about the device, but I could not talk to police about it or email it to them. Also, the police weren't too good at listening to me as they were coming to the consensus, they didn't see it, so then it was a false report and that there was no need for further investigation of the pole that had the device.

I said there was something behind my house, but it was earlier and it was not seen by them.

I sent my father an email with a picture of a device that was an electromagnetic device on a post behind his house. They probably did not understand it happened two days before they inspected the pole.

I believe it was too late for them to reverse that it was false report, and since I did not come out of my house, they started firing tear gas into the house and had a SWAT team drag me out of the house. The police really need to have someone who can talk about the reports rather than assume it's false and drag someone out of their house and destroy it.

My father talked with the police before they broke into the house and tried to tell them I was not a danger to himself or anyone else and forwarded the email I sent to the police. They did not believe either one of us and thought I was making bombs for some reason.

After they broke into the house, they found no guns or bomb-making material. They didn't know they had made a mistake. They then arrested me for making two false reports for talking twice to the police about the device.

If I had left the electromagnetic device on the post, it would not have been a false report, but I thought I was doing the right thing by reporting it and removing it.

The Department of Homeland Security says you should report anything suspicious to the police and that some of the reports may be mistakes or classified devices but we should report them anyway. The

Department of Homeland Security should say if it is a government-made device, then you can be arrested because they might be classified. If their classified and unclassified later in jail, you are supposed to be classified in jail and then you can tell their state psychologist the story which I did. I would not have got arrested if I could have talked to a psychologist before I tried to talk to the police. The state psychologist could even tell how I got arrested and he believed my story, and I was evaluated and found to be competent and did not need to go to the state hospital since my story wasn't crazy. The people that see the state psychologist and did something stupid to get arrested, no matter how normal they act that can't make up for how they were arrested, and they are called incompetent which gets involuntary hospitalization.

Anyway, here is where we are now. We have all learned from this situation. After a lot of work on this, my father was able to buy me another house. I am seeing another nurse practitioner and doctor and taking my medication and all the necessary supplements for all of these human health conditions many people start to get in their twenties to end of life.

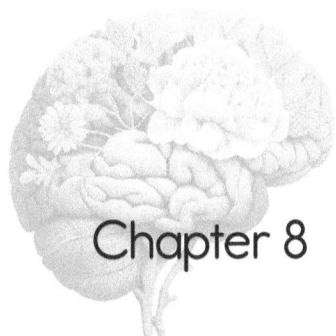

Chapter 8

Conditional Release Treatment and Medical Compliance

I n the eyes of a doctor, nurse, or forensic case manager, if the person can live in the community without any help from them, that's something which should help get them off conditional release. I think that conditional release is like a ramp to something else, and it'll be interesting to see how it'll go with the unconditional release with the new healthcare directives we have with other people who are NGRI. I now have the nurse practitioners' directives and my own healthcare directives and have been doing it with the help of my father.

In my case, I had a psychiatrist that retired about five years ago. I had been seeing that psychiatrist for twenty-five years. When he retired, he did not put me under the care of another one or make a final change from my original diagnosis, so it wasn't good.

Some psychiatrists are unable to diagnose any schizophrenic patients in remission. It is wrong for a psychiatrist not to say a person has their schizophrenia in remission if they are living a normal life.

You can see a nurse and doctor and discuss going to unconditional release, but it is very difficult to make it happen. Some of the NGRIs never get out their conditional release their whole life. This is due to their not being functionally independent in the community, productive, or not very gainful in their living and no support system.

For a person who has already been in psychiatric care for a long time, who knows mental health and has a support system termination is a lot easier. I like having insight into mental illness and substance abuse (SA) and treatment. Also, medication compliance with support help from my parents while having my illness in remission. In remission means it's in remission, and I'm not psychotic and know what's going on and I am doing fine. I'm doing this myself with help from my father.

I have insight into mental illness and SA and full support from my dad, and I had no violations or no relapses into mental illness. As long as I stayed on my prescribed medicine and all my other nutritional supplements and alkaline water, I can function well.

My case worker and judge know I am a previously diagnosed mentally ill person. I told them about my illness going back to when I was twenty. The judge and the case manager know my story and all the current and old issues. Hopefully, they are now trying to decide what to do next. I am not sure if they will do it for anyone else, but I believe I am ready for unconditional release. We're fully separated from our case workers they blocked the phones so now we should terminate the case to fully separate. It's been almost four and a half years since I've been put on conditional release, and that is the average length people stay on it, so it's all about time. Termination is the ultimate goal of the forensic case manager. They should see I will continue with my good behavior after the judge terminates the conditional release.

If you were not guilty by reason of insanity and determined to be competent and as long as you stay on the prescribed medication, then the main objective of the case manager whose job it is to make sure you stay on your medication and you have set up the proper support mechanism to stay well. I believe I have done this and hope that my case manager sees the progress I have made.

I do have a goal, and that is to get off this conditional release. I guess my main flaw is that I am persistent in expressing this to my case manager, but that persistence is also helping me to do everything I need to do to prove I am ready to get off conditional release.

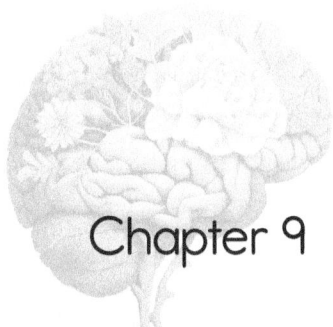

Chapter 9

My Goals Going Forward

The Patient

Things seem to turn out well for those that do good. I hope that my conditional release will be terminated at our next hearing. I will no longer have any conditions of freedom, and I am under no court order anymore. I will still see my doctor, but it will be easier when it's over. Seeing a doctor is easier. I have been doing it for a long time now. I don't need a court order to do it. It's good to know your scores on your blood work so you can tell what you want to do to help yourself.

I have been taking both my doctor's medications, but then I picked up on more things that my primary care doctor was trying to help me with. Doctors know that by eating a high-fat diet, low-carb diet and getting some sunlight in every day helps a lot of inflammation and other problems from eating a high-fat diet.

I also want to focus on my nutrition and get exercise and sunlight and not succumb to these diseases and stay ahead of it. Be wary of too much food from plants and vegetables and eat that in moderation also along with food supplements.

Plants and vegetables don't want you to eat them, and they have natural chemical defense mechanisms; plants are also used for making supplements containing these natural impurities. There are chemicals found naturally in plants and vegetables because plants don't want you to eat them and that's how they protect themselves from predators. Most of the vegetables and most all plants also draw upon a complex arsenal of small-molecule chemical defenses, including terpenoids, alkaloids, phenylpropanoids, glucosinolates, lipids, and nonprotein amino acids. Volatiles which can alert neighbor plants or tissues to potential attacks are promoted by herbivory and are a complex blend.

Vegetables contain naturally occurring defensive chemicals that are designed to harm creatures that try to feast upon them. These chemicals are very toxic to living cells; however, the concentrations that exist in most types of whole vegetables may be relatively safe for most people to eat in moderation and also the supplements because they contain them too. Everybody is better off paying for some of their own healthcare and treating their own cancer and anti-aging CVD, blood pressure, and cardiovascular diseases after they see a doctor first. The maker of Immusist died, and I found I no longer needed Immusist to deal with preventing cancer. I use brown seaweed and treat it with alkaline water and Willard water now instead. For anti-aging, I like Nicotinamide Riboside and NMN for anti-aging and fucoidans, which is brown seaweed, and more I will mention in a later chapter. I also like lots of omega-3 with vitamin B complex and CoQ10 since that is known to prevent cardiovascular disease. The self-healthcare advice I have here is good for mental health, diabetes overweight and metabolic syndrome which everyone gets after their 50. To live past sixty-five, I would have to get on both the anti-aging and preventative cancer fronts and cardiovascular and T2D reversing the illnesses.

Here is a little lesson on aging and why I take these anti-aging supplements. AMPK activator supplements and the common NRF2 nuclear factor erythroid 2 cardiovascular response mechanism control cellular resistance to oxidants by activating an array of antioxidant element- dependent genes. Some of these activators include supplements such as spirulina, sulforaphane made with broccoli seeds and curcumin to help with CVD, anti-aging, diabetes, high blood pressure, cancer, and more. Some other good things to eat is nutritional powder like fiber, green food, collagen peptides, spirulina, and beet root powder. Powder supplements like these prevent high blood pressure, cardiovascular disease, cancer, T2D.

I do use my own supplements and medicines for my own body, however, I have been doing it for a long time since early nineties, and I have gotten better at it. It is a learning curve which I have achieved. I know what needs to be ordered, and I do resupply the supplements and other healthcare items I need if I'm out of one that my body actually needs to stay healthy and to be in compliance within normal healthcare standards exactly what I needed. Also since I have my own living will with this document, I must take orders from Nurse Ted from Stewart-Marchman which is a conditional release rule I'm following still from court. However, I don't need anything else from any other doctor but Ted from Stewart-Marchman; he orders my blood tests to see how well I'm doing from the results. So far the results were not bad. I had expected everything it marked in my blood and I'm treating it and I'm on a very low-carb high-ketogenic diet to fix my insulin resistance.

Vegetables contain naturally occurring defensive chemicals that are designed to harm creatures that try to feast upon them. These chemicals are very toxic to living cells, however, the concentrations that exist in most types of whole vegetables may be relatively safe for most people to eat in moderation, also the supplements because they contain them too.t

Plants are also used for supplements and by eating too many vegetables that contain chemicals because the plants don't want you to eat them, most of the vegetables and most all plants also draw upon a complex arsenal of small-molecule chemical defenses including terpenoids, alkaloids, phenylpropanoids, glucosinolates, lipids, and nonprotein amino acids. Volatiles which can alert neighbor plants or tissues to potential attacks are promoted by herbivory and are a complex blend that contain naturally occurring defensive chemicals that are designed to harm creatures that try to eat them.

You can get high prolactin from taking antipsychotics and that happens because typical antipsychotics block dopamine inhibition of the pituitary and cause the prolactin to go up. Secretion of prolactin by the pituitary is under inhibitory control via dopamine from the hypothalamus. Interference with dopamine secretion by blocking D2 receptors or actions leads to an increase in prolactin. By increasing prolactin production and the prolactin itself enhances the secretion of dopamine so this creates a negative feedback loop. There is too much dopamine from too much prolactin resulting with a higher prolactin level. An easy way to stop the secretion of more dopamine from a higher prolactin level from the negative feedback loop would be to lower the prolactin level by renormalizing the dopamine production in the hippocampus by stopping dopamine inhibition caused by the in Vega and lowering the negative feedback loop going on. High prolactin is one of the major causes of high blood pressure. Furthermore, high blood pressure caused by high prolactin and from not relieving the negative feedback loop going by not lowering my medication can be a cause of kidney damage because the high blood pressure causes kidney damage. My previously diagnosed illness is in remission.

We have senescent cells which are cells that can't replicate anymore also called zombie cells and they produce CD38 which causes inflammation and kills NAD+, the natural anti-aging coenzyme, and CD38 which causes inflammation. Coming from senescent cells come this CD38 that destroys NAD+ but also that can be blocked by taking apigenin to block CD38. Then you can take fucoidans which are brown seaweed to kill off the remaining senescent cells. The senescent cells aren't totally bad but have been known to cause cancer cardiovascular which is the inflammation. Senescent cells also makes the good surrounding cells around the senescent cells cause inflammation. So you could get brown seaweed to kill some of the senescent cells by apoptosis. Less senescent cells increase the amount of NAD+ and decreasing inflammation by having less CD38 from the senescent cells. Less CD38 will be produced with taking brown seaweed and the apigenin to block remaining CD38 and this will boost NAD+ by reducing the CD38 from all the senescent cells. The brown seaweed stops the senescent cells from harming good cell by killing the zombie cells. The taking of brown seaweed to stop the zombie cells from making more senescent cells if you take some which does the senescent therapy which helps anti-aging and preventing cancer and prevents cardiovascular disease and loss of NAD+ found in the body which causes aging. Also, by taking NAD+ precursors supplements nicotinamide riboside and/or NMN and this deals with the senescent cells best. Also, by supplementing your nine essential amino acids you can be sure you get all nine essential amino acids not made in the body and you need to make the body produce all the proteins it needs. The nine essential aminos include histamine, isoleucine, leucine, lysine, methionine, phenylalanine, threonine, tryptophan, and valine and the other twenty are made in the body. All these supplements listed above will cost you around 800 dollars for about three months' supply. It would boost your body functioning and prevent healthcare problems if you did it and you can do this. Wouldn't you want it to protect yourself and stay in top health in the hard times we're in?

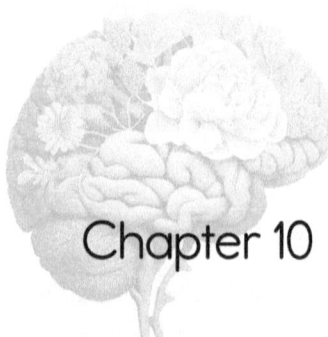

Chapter 10

Family's Goals Going Forward

The Family

I remember when I got interested in helping myself with my father. I had to change my father's goals about nutrition sooner to save ourselves from dying.

I think one big goal was to write this book. Anyone can read it and avoid making some of the mistakes we have made. It will help to avoid repeating mistakes.

Looking back, I remember trying to help my dad to try to help stop my mom from dying from her medicines. Two years before she died, she got colon cancer and had over twelve hours of surgery to get rid of all the cancer. She knew she had cancer but did not want to let them operate on that and wished to die naturally but my dad was persistent and so are doctors to remove the cancer they found in her colon.

It took several months to recover from her colon cancer with exercise, oxygen, and also weight gain. She was down to 90 lbs. Dad was able to get her up to 120 pounds and off oxygen. We thought she was on her way to recovery. All the cancer was gone, but she still had scleroderma and also she was still taking her cholesterol and high blood pressure pills which were prescribed by her doctor.

Scleroderma is a disease which has your body manufacturing too much collagen. She was on blood pressure and cholesterol drugs which are both bad drugs for the reasons below.

She was not on any supplements and maybe one of the things which would have lengthen her life more was to drink a lot of alkaline water that's like a powerful antioxidant. Alkaline water and nutrients rather than cholesterol and high blood pressure medicines. Another way to lower blood pressure is to do stimulation of the vagus nerve. The vagus nerve is a nerve that goes from the brain stem down your throat and down the middle into the stomach and goes back into the heart. When you stimulate the vagus nerve, it helps the heart control stress and balance the sympathetic and parasympathetic nervous system and that would lower blood pressure immediately a lot faster; you can try it yourself by massaging your throat in the middle, and in the lower inside earlobes, it works but that is not as effective as a small device they make called a sensate 2. The sensate 2 puts ultrasound frequency into the vagus nerve and also stimulates it and calms you down. That would be one thing you could get to raise pH of alkaline water mixed with another additive to raise the pH and add Dr. Willard's, Willard water, and also take CoQ10 and don't lower your LDL cholesterol with any drug. Doing that only lowers the good LDL, and you want to lower the oxidized LDL small oxidized particles; that's what causes the inflammation. It helps your health to practice breathing exercises and reduce stress causing the inflammation and to lower blood pressure. By breathing in four seconds and exhaling five seconds slowly helps relax the body and help blood pressure naturally. Breathing in slow and exhaling slower works best to helps neuro plasticity and that trains the brain to help heal the body and alleviate stress. If your blood pressure still remains high after all of the above, then you should do what you doctors says and take your high blood pressure pills. Always follow your doctor's orders since he knows your body and what works.

Drink alkaline water pH water filters pitchers to lower the effects on cholesterols and lower the amounts of oxidized LDL (oxLDL) particles by using antioxidant alkaline water.

Regular LDL cholesterol normal however you have to know oxidized LDL-p is bad which is caused by oxidative stress or sugar. The right blood test for low-density lipoprotein particle (LDL particle or LDL-P), not regular LDL, it's the oxidized LDL also called LDL-p and HDL-p and LDL-C, it's these three cholesterols are what clog or foam up the arteries with inflammation. They use the nuclear magnetic resonance NMR test for this. LDL-p particles are created from your body having stress, oxidative stress, high insulin, high blood sugar. The old system could test LDL-P also it is what diabetics have to check as the root cause of cardiovascular disease. Statin drugs cause deficiencies in cholesterol and CoQ10 and only take out the good LDL, but not the bad LDL-P cholesterol. Therefore, statins make no difference in preventing cardiovascular disease even though they lower LDL statins can increase the risk of heart problems by statins stopping the production of CoQ10 and cholesterol in the body which are both necessary nutrients for the heart. Doing that only lowers the good LDL and you want to lower the oxidized LDL small oxidized particles; that's what causes the inflammation.

Chapter 11

What Needs to be Done in
the Medical Industry

The Family

According to a university research, the mental illness is among the most common health conditions in the United States. Even though it affects almost every family, it is something that is not focused on enough. People that have any type of mental illness are looked down upon. This should not be happening, and we need to change how we think about people with a mental illness. We also need to focus on curing the different types of mental illness and also focus on how we bring all mental illness into remission.

The actual amount of people living after being diagnosed with mental illness is skewed due to deaths and survival of many of these people. They say only one percent of the population has mental illness; the rest of the previously diagnosed have to live in remission. Millions that experienced mental illness would have it better now in the new system than it was when they were first not diagnosed.

Schizophrenia is a long-term mental disorder of a type involving a breakdown in the relation between thought, emotion, and behavior, leading to faulty perception, inappropriate actions and feelings, withdrawal from reality and personal relationships into fantasy and delusion, and a sense of mental delusions.

There have been great improvements in the medications and supplements as we have better medicine after the old medicines were not that good.

There was another book written by Nicholas Licausi called *The Medical Project*. In that book, they describe a database that should be put together that would detect when diseases start. By doing this, we will be able to find a pattern of what is causing schizophrenia or any other illness. It also describes what are the best things to do if you have an illness or condition. Later in this book, we will discuss the details about a Medical Computer.

If Medical Computer was put together back when COVID started, they could have contained it before it spread and treated it at its origin.

This book also describes the Medical Computer the best treatments for some conditions that can be found. So someone using the Medical Computer once it is complete will know what treatments are the best.

That Medical Computer would be very helpful for someone thinking about getting kids diagnosed with schizophrenia because it would tell us what would be best for the parents with their own families. It would also tell us where the best hospitals are to treat schizophrenia. It would also tell us where the best after care for someone with this illness is and how much does that cost for that treatment.

A long time ago when people started studying what now causes schizophrenia, they did not have supercomputers, the cloud, or the internet. We have it now, so we should be able to compile the data, look for patterns, and find a cure and many other diseases. Now Medicare is running out of money, we really need this Medical Computer because it will lower the cost of everything. You will be able to cure diseases sooner before they spread, doctors will be able to determine the best cures for illnesses before they get worse, and you will be able to help yourself with diabetes and other illnesses. The government or some rich person must put together the Medical Computer because it will reduce medical cost by stopping viruses from spreading and catching illnesses when they first start.

We need a Medical Computer that would help patients and doctors both at the same time with schizophrenia. Having a mental health computer requires homework. A young adult might need to sit on the couch and think and help buy their own food and supplements to live at home with their dad and mom and not fight and have new medicine in the house to cure all the diseases mentioned here in this book themselves.

The reason I was diagnosed with schizophrenia was my parents took me to a drug testing center and I had been smoking pot and I tested positive for pot. After that happened, my parents took me to a psychologist, and my parents told her I was using drugs and we had someone in our family that was schizophrenic. The psychologist recommended my parents should send me to a mental hospital. Maybe if we had the Medical Computer, then I could have read that smoking pot could lead to schizophrenia, especially if someone in your family is already schizophrenic. I would have never smoked pot.

Being a young adult would only be good if you were living with your parents and staying home and staying healthy. This may not be the best approach for staying out of trouble and good. Additionally, there has always been a problem with what needs to be done after a person leaves the hospital with some parents. In some cases, the family can take care of the ill person. Sharing money and things must be worked on as early as possible because you need money for new support system living in the house again with your parents.

That's okay; it's not just about us since it's about mental health and self-help, but one more thing, some people who did mental health who did do it with me, they don't all take care of things the same or have the same fruits of the labor or might not be successful with their treatments or are not as serious. This also happens with people of all ages, and it could be anyone despite their age. This also ruins doing a healthcare system by age since we don't get better at the same time; we talked about remission and the government still has problems with doing healthcare by age. Anyway, you wouldn't want an old man to have to do healthcare like he did when he was as a kid if he was already in remission for sixteen years. There should be so much less control for them if they thought about each of the different people, but people are different. I don't care if this book has a central idea for mental health by age; that would be like a hotel having a specific receptionist for each specific person, but I don't live in the Holiday Inn. However, this book doesn't need to be about just our family since we're helping others. It could be about many others; it is not just me.

In our case, the first hospital sometimes let people out as soon as their insurance ran out. In my case, I was able to stay for a while, but after a certain period, my family and I had to pay for some of my stay in the hospital. Some places had way less control over helping when there was less money, not using the best hospital to save money when there are money issues or insurance problems.

I was lucky my parents had good insurance, and when the coverage was reduced, my family could afford to pay. After I left, I asked where I could go after the hospital, and they mentioned an Orlando residential treatment center. Instead of doing that right then, I got an apartment near the hospital where I became an outpatient in the same hospital.

Depending on the person that is ill and their family, maybe they can live together instead of separating like I did. But in my case, that was not possible because my parents didn't want me to stay with them. The main problem is there is training for the family by group therapies at the hospital, but my mother didn't want to attend because the hospital did not do a good job.

The family does not understand the patient with the illness, and it would be best for the person who is ill to live with their family if possible. I also do not believe there should be a hospital that keeps people with schizophrenia if they have place to call home. Most hospitals still have a money problem with keeping patient long-term because of the insurance. In my case, my parents and I had trouble living together after I was first diagnosed. We loved each other and would have liked to have lived together, but we have been split apart due to parents' wishes. In the first hospital, there should have been a home living program put in place that would train families how to live with someone with schizophrenia.

When I left that hospital, I was not put on any medication after I got out. I tried to ask my doctor if I could keep seeing him after I got out, but he said no because he had a stack of paperwork on me already that he showed me. Since that first hospital, I have been in and out of many hospitals and also jail. After being released from jail and put on conditional release, I was put on metformin, and I studied insulin-resistant T2D by watching webinars. I was working on a diet of Nutritional Ketosis for weight-loss management and metabolic reversal. I was on a very low-carb ketogenic diet and started to reverse insulin resistance. I discussed with my doctor adding medication like Immusist to take with metformin, and they said take nothing at that time because of the diabetes even though Immusist was good for diabetes.

If we had a Medical Computer as described in *The Medical Project* and later in the book, my own combination of supplements and alkaline water could be tried.

When I was first hospitalized, they had to have a lot of professionals to do the cases right, and they had to pay a lot of money for the staff. You might need to do some stuff yourself. Currently, most places like hospitals are short-staffed and sometimes don't function right or fairly. The hospital I started at ran out of money and had to close.

When you are first diagnosed with a disease, the doctor will give you medicine like you were a beginner because I had no idea of all the different medicines or supplements. Today with YouTube, doctors are talking about curing or preventing diseases on the web. My schizophrenia is in remission, and as long as I take my medication, it will stay in remission.

You need to always work with your parents to determine what is best for you. In my case, I was in remission, but the doctor didn't diagnose me as being in remission.

I have decided to stay on my medicine and many supplements, and my doctor checks my blood work every couple of months to see how I am doing.

Since I have learned a great deal about nutrition, I have the flexibility to take my own best remedies for what my own body needs. My doctor and I check my blood to make sure the combination of supplements and medicines is working properly. A Medical Computer would also have helped in this area with blood work tests.

For my pre-diabetes, I fix that problem with my very low-carb ketogenic diet now. I do this at home with my own food. But other people might not fix their food or take supplements so they would need to take the doctor's medicine. I prefer to fix the disease in the most advanced way possible using the most efficient methods. I do this with my doctor's supervision.

I take over twenty-five supplement pills each morning to fix pre-diabetes, blood pressure, anti-aging, CVD, and schizophrenia. The only disease I use a doctor for is to treat the schizophrenia, but I do check with other doctors to make sure my other illnesses stay normal.

I recommend curing pre-diabetes and high blood pressure with the support of a doctor and a very low-carb ketogenic diet. I am also trying to fix depression and high blood pressure by taking NAC, serine and glycine, NMN, and doing exercise.

I did get myself checked to make sure my pre-diabetes and high blood pressure stayed normal. There are no better medicines than these. However, the best medicine for schizophrenia is what the doctor has prescribed for you.

I am happy to be in my shoes today because I now have insight into mental health and substance abuse and these other illnesses. The case worker might think I have wisdom in these areas.

I developed this insight at the treatment centers, and you get insight for this by doctors helping you and you helping yourself. It takes most people about two years to start getting this insight. You develop this insight with your doctors and thinking about medicines for what your body needs. The Medical Computer would allow you and your doctors to develop this insight sooner and spread the best practices worldwide if they changed the whole healthcare system as described in the book *The Medical Computer* by Nicholas Licausi.

Now, after they put a lot of money into the last treatment center I was at, it's like a different place and it was quite expensive.

In two or three years of living there, you could have bought a house with the money instead. But I guess some rich disabled people want to develop this insight, so they go there.

Now I'm at another treatment center as a patient. Hopefully, my case managers will soon see that I understand my own problems and will continue to take care of myself. Also, they will understand that I have this insight into mental illness.

The forensic case manager is looking for somebody to be my case worker right now. Usually, they hire somebody that quits right away. I have had eight of them so far and they just found me a new one.

It is important to educate our case workers and judges in this area on a medical computer. We all have a big responsibility in working with the mentally ill who have an NGRI.

I have another hearing coming, and I have a new case worker that just met me. It has been almost four years by the time it started the next time I see the judge.

Each time I get a new case worker, I go through the whole story of how I got into this situation. I have described this before in the book, but with a new case worker, I have all the information written down to update them.

The story I start with I described earlier in the book and below.

We are told on the Department of Homeland Security website that if you see something like a device or bomb, then it is your duty to say something to the police. That is what I was trying to do. I was not aware that I had to investigate myself only to see if the device or bomb was really still there and that the police had to see it there, but if it wasn't there, I would be giving a false report. I was unaware of this when I removed the device and then reported the device in my backyard. The Department of Homeland Security was created after 9-11 in 2002, and they recommended if you see something, say something but don't call Homeland Security; you're supposed to call the police, and for a long time before 2002, the police are used to not asking for the details like who or what it was, or when, where, or why it looked suspicious. Also if they didn't actually see it themselves since I removed it even as matter of fact, it's very hard to prove it took place after the fact. My problem and the police's problems were that we were not able to differentiate about the facts of the device's existence and the evidence and leads I gave them, which led to their false reports. Also, when my family talked with the police at 1 a.m., we did not communicate well with them.

They tell criminal justice students in high school and colleges if they report a device or bomb, and they didn't see it; it's false, and they should not trust anyone but themselves without further investigation. Furthermore, if a lot of devices or explosions went off and the police didn't see or hear it, the people that saw it and reported it would all get taken to jail. Also, this activity is a weakness in humans because they can't do anything about devices or explosions in a normal way without escalating the situation. Judges are not allowed to drop a false report of bomb or explosion charge even if there are two charges of it and one was classified and kept a secret, I don't think you would want talk at all about anything classified even to police anything that could send you to prison for life or even get an NGRI, which is not easy for talking about it.

We are all told today to report anything suspicious by Homeland Security, and that is what I was doing. There seems to be a problem with the police understanding people who are trying to report something. They have to be informed the 4Ws right from the beginning, who or what, when, where, and why it's important, and they have to know all four usually, but if it's something like a frequency device that can kill you and it is classified, you're in trouble reporting it; you should move out of the area even if it's a house, or run in the bathroom.

The adult children would also need support and/or acceptance from their own families and the community.

In my case, how would the police assume to know that someone knows that they lied to them already without investigation and the police give me a false report charge based on a thrown-away photo? I believe there was a device in my backyard that would harm me and others, and I still have the picture of the device which I gave to them then. I did not lie about that, but I may not have communicated that it was removed already.

I know people have complained about the police need more help in criminal justice in this false reporting area and in racism. I may have been one of the people that has suffered due to a improper investigation by the police. I reported something that was misconstrued.

It would have been interesting if I decided to bring this case to trial and had a lawyer not taken a plea of not guilty due to insanity. My family and I did not want to get a lawyer to save money, and we thought the public defender was good. Also, we did not want to take a chance on a jury trial because if I lost, then I would be in prison. Maybe that was a mistake, and now I am on conditional release.

Based on some studies concerning pot use and schizophrenia, I may have been diagnosed with schizophrenia at that time because of substance abuse, but now the schizophrenia is in remission.

At the time, I was on pot, a substance regulated by the government; they didn't have any medical marijuana until around 2015. Back then, I was diagnosed with schizophrenia from substance abuse, which was interchangeable with schizophrenia just because people get help with both. I got both help and lived separated from my mom and dad with schizophrenia in remission most of my life from about twenty-six years old to the present. This is another reason we need a Medical

Computer. We know that some people can smoke pot and not develop schizophrenia, but others develop psychosis. We need to see if there is a pattern so we can advise people about not using pot which may cause psychosis.

Based on the information we have, we know that many people who smoke pot do not develop schizophrenia. One theory would be that some people could be in a good place environmentally when they are smoking. Maybe some people are already in a bad place environmentally when they smoke and do that too much. It is a good idea not to smoke street pot anytime while you are alive. If you do smoke, then make sure you get a medical marijuana doctor and don't go into a psychosis; if you do go into a psychosis, then stop smoking it.

I believe if you're diagnosed with schizophrenia, stay on your medicine, and if you think you are in remission, make sure you stay on your medicine so it stays in remission. The doctor that retired told me to seek newer counselors and talk to them about moving to another house. I tried, and then nothing happened, and more stuff happened. More bad things will happen to you if your support system does not know about your doctor's suggestions.

He never told my parents about that session, and I wish he did. He could see I was having a problem at that house which could not have all been due just to my neighbor's things. It took a lot of changing over a lot of places I had to go, but now I'm back home in the same community I was but not the same street. I am sure that if I stay very productive, I have the ability to take care of my new house.

I believe wellness has to be worked on to achieve it. My schizophrenia medicine isn't a bad thing to take, but it can't help unless you know the causes of it and other diseases. I will explain these other factors.

Reasons for schizophrenia causes and early dementia are multifactorial but reversible by having insight into mental health, if any substance abuse, and functioning independently, productive, sense of empowerment, overcoming feelings of internalized stigma.

When I was diagnosed with schizophrenia, they did not know how pot and schizophrenia are related. I think today they know it can cause psychosis in some people but not all people.

One of the reasons we need the Medical Computer is to review the work that was done concerning pot and schizophrenia. Paul, who became a psychiatrist, did smoke pot, and he did not get schizophrenia, but recently, pot and psychosis were linked, so this can be a factor that can lead to schizophrenia.

Other factors contributing to worsening mental illness include environmental, psychological abuse, intellectual or physical abuse. Also, it's caused by degenerative diseases in older adults that are more biologically created than psychologically or intellectually and by not knowing about what you are doing. Early dementia cases often result in schizophrenia also and the early symptoms of mental decline and may be made less severe by preventing or by fixing hearing loss, traumatic brain injury, obesity, hypertension, alcohol, T2D, social isolation, less education, depression, insulin resistance, sedentary, diabetes, stress, and air and water pollution, and it's when and if any of these twelve things are present that can trigger early dementia to get worse.

The Medical Computer will contain all studies that are done related to all of these diseases all over the world. This would allow someone in any city in the world to be aware of any work related to any illness like schizophrenia, cancer, etc.

The Medical Computer can also help people that are evaluating people with schizophrenia because it will be able to tell that person what would determine if the schizophrenia is in remission.

In determining an illness, the Medical Computer would match the symptoms, known issues, and actions with known causes of the disease. Medical Computer should let them know if they need a pre-diagnosed supplement. Then the Medical Computer could determine exactly what type of problems they face and possible solutions to try and fix their issues if there are any that they can try at home or in a clinic.

Due to costs and saving freedom, people should try to mimic the treatments doctors use, and that way the Medical Computer can help people who don't yet have a disease or previously diagnosed diseases but want to do something to help themselves both patients and doctors. The Medical Computer can recommend I take a drug for a previously diagnosed disease or just keep it in remission.

But if I'm at risk for some disease but don't have it like cancer, the Medical Computer could recommend something else like a senolytic supplement like brown seaweed or omega-3 without a diagnosis of a disease. I'm at risk for cancer because of my polluted air and water, but don't have it yet but the environment is known to cause it.

Also, the Medical Computer should tell the person using new system data what the persons can eat at home if the patient has T2D and supplement and foods or it can be dangerous. Instead of diagnosing pre-type-2 diabetes, a diagnosis of insulin resistance and treat metabolic syndrome that I mentioned in later chapters.

I treat insulin resistance but not the way the doctors treat type-2 diabetes now. I do a very low-carb ketogenic diet on a rotating interval with a regular whole food keto diet. Maybe a Medical Computer will be a useful tool for this diet for all doctors and people.

Also, the case manager and judge need the Medical Computer and the programming for conditional release plan criteria for understanding the removal of conditions. Case managers have to know if they already modified the conditional release plan for the patient and who accepts their mental illness and takes responsibility for it and gets a sense of empowerment.

The Medical Computer and case managers and clinicians would have to know by Medical Computer data if the patient does not need involuntary hospitalization by imputing their current and prior commitments to a mental hospital and if they have completed treatment and their successes in the community.

Also, the Medical Computer can save patient data for a doctor for people who don't need conditions at all where they stay and can have unconditional living.

This is because they would already be in the community on their own because they completed the original conditional release plan modification with their successful independent living in the community. After these, people complete the successful modified conditional release plan and are successful in the community meeting the original conditions of their own homes criteria.

The Medical Computer could also be used for previously diagnosed mental patients who don't require involuntary commitments because they don't fit the original conditions or illness severity they had before they were put in the hospitals and then were sent back to their home in their community if it's possible. The Medical Computer could save many lives and help many people keep their freedoms. They won't have to get hospitalized so they can go to outpatient medication management clinics from home and supplementations without commitment to mental hospitals.

Building the Medical Computer would take a joint government project and cost a lot of money and time, but would stop a lot of problems in our country.

Doing these things I just mentioned would bring us closer to the reality of getting a Medical Computer because we need people doing it to build a consensus and computer database and insight needed for knowledge of living a meaningful life.

If the parents won't support adult children because of some problems, then it's a problem. This is because if your adult children are in remission permanently or not, they would still need some permanent support similar to social security from their parents. The adult children could get something going on in the community to make money and help pay their bills. Your treatment success has to work with families in the communities, so adult children working and living with their parents need to be considered before becoming a parent especially if this disease runs in your family.

Sometimes the statistical errors for an undiagnosed schizophrenic who is in remission are understated by social workers and medical experts to know if they are following the right rules and the constitution.

As a recovered mental patient or undiagnosed ones, the adult children should be supported by their parents and that way they can help their parents support them by working and help buy food.

Many have built a consensus that vitamins and supplements mentioned in this book are going to react chemically to their one drug from their doctor, but the vitamins and supplements are safe to take. Proceed carefully with all your healthcare endeavors. Do your own research on the web. Also check with your doctors to make sure it's okay to take the medication with the supplements.

One possible solution for schizophrenia that was tried years ago, which did not work, was to put all people with schizophrenia in involuntary hospitalization. When the medicines for schizophrenia improved, they found that they were necessary to get better. Also, it was determined that the people in the hospital, in some cases, were misdiagnosed upon leaving the hospital. Their treatments and therapies were also good at the residential treatment centers.

That approach was probably not easier on the families. In some cases, the person with the illness lives without the family, and when the mother and father die, the person either becomes homeless or is put in a clinic.

The psychiatrist I had when I was in the FEMA jail was the only one that said my illness was in remission. The government has a different protocol for military and FEMA psychiatrists who are in the only government spot that had remission status after thirty-five years of seeing outside doctors. This protocol of diagnosing in remission should be blended into our regular society not just keep saying they're in remission only in FEMA jails but with all other doctors included using the same protocols.

My state of mind was the same when I got out of jail but then, when I got out, the nurse practitioner said it was not in remission because that psychiatrist was not working for the same company even though it was the same company. Therefore, doctors should use the term *remission* the same. That is one thing a Medical Computer will fix. You will have a common set of definitions to describe something.

The jail doctor was right by diagnosing me being in remission, but that was the one time that they are right, and I never had a doctor say that before. Remission was a good diagnosis, and therefore we're eligible for more therapies. I did not receive other therapies since the doctors did not agree after I got out with that doctor.

This would not occur with the medical computer because it always gives the right diagnosis. So would a tele-psychiatrist you can get yourself right now you can do at your own home.

During the COVID epidemic, they developed the first database on a medical computer using electronic records and scientific facts about curing COVID. The Medical Computer we are talking about would be similar, only it would contain cures or recommendations for all unknown or known diseases.

A study published in *Personality and Individual Differences* suggests that some people reject the COVID-19 vaccine. The Medical Computer would not be able to fix this. But patients should have rights to their own body.

Often people don't research what their doctor's medicines are doing in their bodies or what their medicines are about. Medicine is for your failing health problems, and the Medical Computer will describe this in detail. It would be best if you had the intuition to get the best medicine for yourself by researching; that becomes a part of what you understand by reading this book.

Healthcare and helping yourself is a learning curve, and it's to reduce the burden to doctors if you do some things yourself. You can save money by doing this, and also reduce your bill. The Medical Computer will be able to bill the appropriate Medicare, insurance, or person for any service. This service might not be needed or might be available sometime.

A Medical Computer can do healthcare or finish cases faster and help undiagnosed people faster by using the Medical Computer using remission to help the community better and healthcare industry. You should always get your healthcare faster for remission of mental illness as an outpatient because outpatients usually don't get in as much trouble. Caseworkers, counselors, and doctors can do their treatment plan using the Medical Computer.

Most people start to develop neurological cardiovascular and heart diseases, which are preventable by taking supplements daily like fish oil or omega-3 and CoQ10, K2, Nitric Oxide precursors, and brown seaweed and alkaline water. Also, if you have high blood pressure, take these supplements, which I just mentioned, and they are the best you can take. These supplements are good for me, but you might need a living will healthcare directive to control your wishes if you want to refuse a physician's care. There also needs to be in the computer about reversing metabolic syndrome information.

I don't like blood pressure drugs because they lower your blood pressure in the short term but can cause heart problems later and even death. Taking nitric oxide precursors like L-arginine and NAC and serin can lower blood pressure better and fix the problems caused by taking blood pressure medicines themselves, which cause other long-term damage any time you change how an organ like the heart functions.

Hypertension is a major risk factor for cardiovascular disease, and the reduction of elevated blood pressure significantly reduces the risk of cardiovascular events. Endothelial dysfunction, which is characterized by impairment of nitric oxide (NO) bioavailability, is an important risk factor for both hypertension and cardiovascular disease and may represent a major link between the conditions. Evidence suggests that nitric oxide plays a major role in regulating blood pressure and that impaired nitric oxide bioactivity is an important component of hypertension. N-acetyl cysteine (NAC) is a supplement form of cysteine.

Consuming adequate cysteine and NAC is important for a variety of health reasons, including replenishing the most powerful antioxidant in your body, glutathione. These amino acids also help with chronic respiratory conditions, fertility, and brain health.

Smoking can be very bad and can change your lung functionality and decrease your lifespan, and the blood pressure goes higher, and your teeth fall out, but that's not all it does. Smoking causes your body to age sooner. If you want to live better and longer, don't smoke, so I take nicotine lozenges every day instead, and I've been doing that permanently since nicotine binds to can slow the healing of damaged tissues that are in the body. The nicotine lozenges I buy are from Amazon, and Amazon produces the nicotine lozenges themselves. They worked, and I was taking them instead of smoking cigarettes. but then I stopped. Other things I like are anti-aging. I use NMN and nicotinamide riboside together because they help regulate the body's genetic functions to not make errors. If your genetic function makes errors such as activating a liver cell response in your brain, that can be bad. Taking NMN and nicotinamide riboside helps with preventing this since it activates sirtuins. I take both supplements. Some people take one or the other but taking both gives you more of it in your blood to help the genetic functioning. Serine is a non-essential amino acid in humans. It produces glycine and from supplementing with serine and functionally important in many proteins. With an alcohol group, serine is needed for the metabolism of fats, fatty acids, and cell membranes; muscle growth; and a healthy immune system. Taking NAC Serin and NAD+ together can help take care of oxidative stress and help with CVD, blood pressure, T2D, and prevent aging and cancer.

You already have enough sugar in your body that is made in your liver which is all you need to survive. You should never let your sugar stay too high. My fasting blood glucose is usually elevated, but my A1C is close to normal. So, to correct this, I only eat one meal a day. I never eat carbs or sugary drinks or diet drinks. Diet drinks and fake sugar can increase the insulin amounts in your blood, which will worsen your insulin resistance. Even diet stuff is bad for diabetes, so you should not eat it because it increases insulin resistance, and you want to be insulin sensitive. You should drink plenty of water also, and they make a water additive called double helix that changes the surface tension of water, which makes the water absorbed into the blood cells easier. You can get sick and malnourished if you don't drink enough alkaline water remineralized with prenatal nutrients such as Dr. Willard's Willard water and mix it in a pH water filter pitcher.

Insulin sensitivity is necessary to absorb insulin and glucose. You can take something for that, such as apple cider vinegar and chromium in most multivitamins. Metformin is also not good to take to lower glucose, and it's not that good to take every day. It would help if you fixed insulin resistance mostly with diet and exercise.

It would be nice to reverse a syndrome that could help people with pre-T2D with the ketogenic diet. Most of the time, the doctor tries to fix just one thing that's wrong, but you need to fix the causes of the diseases caused by other risk factors such as your previous diet. A Medical Computer could tell you to fix that, and in the ways, I mentioned, you could have to do that yourself at home with the new system and the medical computer. Also, the medical computer could recommend supplements to do more things than just one thing the doctor tries to fix diseases in the old system. Many people with mental health conditions can't handle stress as well as others who can, and if you are more rebellious, it can make you look dumber. Often you are thinking about things, or they make it like it's out of your control and stressing you out more, so you should think of something positive instead until you are ready to fix those things that were stressing you out. You can think of positive things that take your mind off the stress, like an inanimate object, or say something else to yourself positive so you can feel in control again. Stressful situations play a major role in making you look less smart and schizophrenic, so you have to go along with it sometimes or think of something else. One further thing that exacerbates the fighting is chemically induced fighting they put chemicals in clouds that cause sinus inflammation and psychological issues with people. You have to keep your nose clean with a Nettie pot or a Navage, which uses saline solution to filter out chemicals from inside the nose which helps stop anxiety and stops fighting from within the family.

People describe mental health as non-life threatening when it is life threatening because of the number of suicides and homicides from being diagnosed. Some mentally ill people are not suicidal, depending on their environment. I think drinking alkaline water and nutritional supplements and a regular whole foods diet is a way to be nicer to your own body. One further problem doing this is big government sending a WARNING LETTER from the FDA about a chemical called immusist. This immusist was very helpful to people and should have continued rather than taken down. The company closed for about a year but reopened with a new product called immusist advance. Immusist advance has better ingredients and has more vitamins in it now.

This is to advise you that the US Food and Drug Administration (FDA) reviewed your website at the Internet address www.immusist. com in August and October 2020 and has determined that you take orders there for the products IMMUSIST Original and IMMUSIST Natural. The claims on your website establish that the products are drugs under section 201(g)(1)(B) of the Federal Food, Drug, and Cosmetic Act (the Act) [21 U.S.C. § 321(g)(1)(B)] because they are intended for use in the cure, mitigation, treatment, or prevention of disease. As explained further below, introducing or delivering these products for introduction into interstate commerce for such uses violates the Act. You can find the Act and FDA regulations through links on FDA's home page at www.fda.gov.

An example of the website claims that provide evidence that your products are intended for use as drugs include the following:

"IMMUSIST™ . . . was formulated by blending certain surfactants with characteristics such as Antivirals, Antifungals . . . and Antibacterials that can . . . reduce inflammation." Your website also contains evidence of intended use in the form of personal testimonials recommending or describing the use of IMMUSIST Original and IMMUSIST Natural products for the cure, mitigation, treatment, or prevention of disease. Examples of such testimonials on the Life Experiences. This website was very helpful to some people and should have continued rather than taken down.

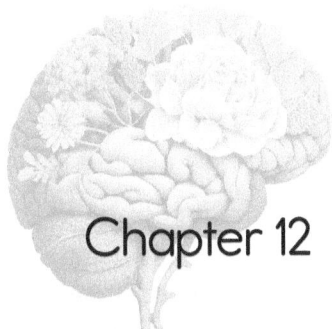

Chapter 12

Mistakes Made in Remission and Recovery

Remission is defined, but Recovery is less precisely defined. However, based on lives, people who have been treated who seem to be in remission and being in the full recovery from schizophrenia usually involves how well they are settled in and secured to their new or old environment, some have had to rebuild a lot out of their old life to get back in, yet others didn't have to rebuild as much of their old lives to live their old life again and some had everything left from their old life while others do not. If their old support systems still willfully support them in their new life after therapy, that's great, also if they are taking enough precautions to have settled in to secure their more productive lives and keep their sense of empowerment if that takes support money and houses or apartments that is ideal and they are lucky. If they gained back everything or not after is what recovered means.

Improvements in either clinical or functional domains need to be seen for at least two years. Moderate quality evidence finds the overall rate of remission is around 36% in people with schizophrenia. I don't think a recovered schizophrenic who's in remission can always make up for the time of lost productivity they lost during the time they were in treatment or the money they lost from the lost productivity. Also in some people with support systems like I have, they required me to get out on own first and pay for that myself before my parents would again support me before they bought me a house and supported me. This is like needing a shoehorn for an apartment for buying a house, and I have seen the same thing happen with others. You have to talk about it all first with the parents or support systems; one thing, time, it took eight years the first time and the next time it took ten months. I had to live with just an average apartment with little support system and then get a good support system again ten months later to be financial independent and depending on the time that takes to save the money can take months to years. With people with first-episode psychosis, the remission percentage is around 58% by 5.5 years. Moderate to low-quality evidence finds rates of remission vary considerably in the developing world, with remission rates by 25 years ranging from 31% in Colombia to 77% in India. India pays 1.14% out of wages for their social security. we pay 6.2% out of our wages for social security, but I don't know how they are diagnosing them to be precise in reality. With a disabled person even a recovered one, there is still a need to keep their federal assistance benefits even if they are actually in remission or recovered which is probable. My doctor never saw me at my house to see if I'm settled and secure or never diagnosed as being in remission or recovered. Furthermore, it's really about how good of a support system they have to support them after they get through treatment or medication management. Most recovery and remission patient status are really linked to a system with social security programs and confidential to the doctor which I could not find out before when I asked him. We know the remission statistics, but I don't know if they are diagnosing them right in the industry. Also, you are talking about millions of people with disability.

Additionally, there is still a need to keep their assistance benefits and their help from their support group. My doctor never saw me at my house to see if I am settled in and in remission. It is important to see my support and how I am functioning.

Before, the mental health industry tries to prevent the loss of revenues from the losses of people within the mental health industry from being in treatment and hospitals and jails. The losses of over a trillion dollars a year of revenues were lost. There should be more focus on being functioning and productive, even if you have a mental health condition. This should be done so the patients can return to being functioning independent and productive, and also have a sense of empowerment and make money themselves and overcame negative feelings and internalized stigma.

Most mental patients diagnosed in remission are capable of learning a trade and possibly starting a business or even writing a book so they can get back to living productive lives. Others could work as a volunteer, such as I did as a cabinet maker's apprentice. I also worked as a daily paid worker, which helped me return to work. This can be done by having groups discuss getting a new job, going back to school, or vocational rehabilitation.

There is always something that anyone can do to help to get involved in their community. Normal people can be driven, productive, and hard-working. Anybody can be considered to be able to be working and, with that said, if they can be capable, God willing, and good productive workers in the public sector and not rely so much on federal assistance programs, but they might not be as useful to do very much. When the medicines for the diseases improved, they found that that was not necessary to get the therapies. Also, it was determined that the people they put in mental hospitals, in some cases, were misdiagnosed again upon leaving the mental hospitals. Their treatments and therapies for other diseases besides schizophrenia were also not that good at residential treatment centers and the expensive mental health centers.

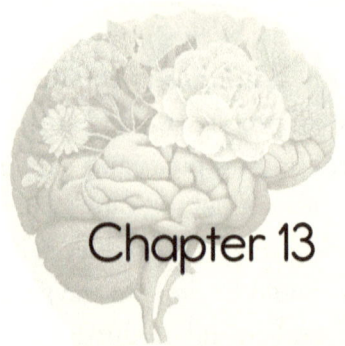

Chapter 13

Medical Computer Restart

The Patient's Responsibilities

The first book is written on this topic called *The Medical Project* by Nicholas Licausi, and it talked about a computer with a worldwide database. This system does not exist today but should be built, and it would allow doctors and patients themselves to benefit worldwide. The end result would allow doctors and patients themselves to see what needs to be done to cure any disease with the medical computer.

Many corporations have put together their version of their corporation cultures along with a database to manage what is going on with doctors and patients. This corporate environment and the end user can be the start of a USA and worldwide corporate medical system.

It will be most difficult to merge these separate corporate systems and add to them since it's important, moving forward, to put together a set of standards to incorporate different corporate systems so it will be easy for these corporations to correlate to each other with bureaucracy for better treatments. Most treatment centers have a corporate adhocracy culture of decentralized leadership, individual leadership, individual initiative, and organic decision-making. Hospitals or treatment centers don't rely on a rigid system of authority or procedures. Instead, they focus on consistently adapting methods by giving employees or patients who are closest to the action permission to do their work and solve problems as they see fit.

When the Medical Computer is put together, it would help people that have any type of illness and recommending all the treatments for that type of illness. It would also give results for those treatments and where people should go to get the best treatment at the best hospital.

The Medical Computer would allow treatments for all known conditions to be more effective and distributed around the world. In addition, if a known disease or virus is detected by the Medical Computer because of the number of illnesses occurring in a particular area, then the computer would set off an alarm to prevent the spread. An example of this would be COVID. COVID would never have spread. The best vaccine and treatment would be developed at that location and entered into the Medical Computer database, and everyone having a Medical Computer would know the best treatment.

Also, when the project is completed and everyone is using it, then no one should be complaining that one person is being treated differently than another person. Doctors will be able to check in the computer to verify that they are providing similar treatments for each patient that has a particular illness. The rich and poor will be getting the same treatment for any illness. It should be announced similarly to the way we announced the space program and putting people on the moon. After about three years, this project could be completed in the United States and then made available to other countries.

This needs to be a worldwide project, starting in the USA. The system would not be as effective if it just was in the USA. You know that if you are having a larger number of doctors inputting ways, they are treating cancer or other illnesses then there is more of a chance to find the best cure. There is a better chance that you will find the right treatments with more doctors inputting data into the Medical Computer.

It is estimated that the number of lives saved per year would be in the millions and the quality of life would be better. Also, a contagion like COVID would never have spread.

Also, this system would find the best cures for any illness. If someone gets sick and a cure for that sickness is found anywhere in the world, it will be shared with anyone that has access to the medical computer.

The project would have five stages and over time the number of lives saved would be increased after each stage is complete and also as the database grows.

The database in the Medical Computer would grow as more patient information is put into the database by adding hospitals, cities, and countries. Right now, we have many hospitals and some cities using different corporate medical systems.

The development team that would put the system together would have six departments. There would be a planning department that would get approvals from doctors, governments, and countries. The Planning Group will be made up of doctors, programmers, engineers, and people that have experience in mental health, cancer, other diseases, and nutrition fields. This group of people will be responsible for researching and deciding if there is a medical computer they can build upon or if we will have to start from the beginning. They will also be responsible for getting all the approvals from doctors and government worldwide.

The doctors, nutritionists, and people that have experience with mental health, cancer, and other illnesses will be key to putting together what results they would like to see as the output from the Medical Computer. This will be based on questions asked and thorough testing to determine an illness during each of the phases.

When this work is complete, an architecture for the Medical Computer would be put together. Then the design would be done.

The first software development department would be developing the front end of the software, which everyone would see. The second software development group would develop all the back-end software which would interface with the database and gather the information.

The fifth department would put together all the test cases and test the Medical Computer. The sixth department would maintain the system after it is released to the world and fix any errors in the Medical Computer once it is in use.

The release of the system will be in five stages, which will start in the USA at hospitals that agreed to be a part of the medical computer initial release. Each stage should be fully tested and working before releasing the next stage.

The first stage would have the doctors or assistants input information into the computer systems. All diagnoses will be made by the doctor and assisted by the Medical Computer. This would mean that once the USA has the system working, it will be released to doctors worldwide.

Based on the information entered, a diagnosis would be recommended by the Medical Computer. If the patient agreed, then the doctor would use that diagnosis. This would be like a second opinion to the doctor. If the doctor did not agree then they would go with their own diagnosis and input that diagnosis in the Medical Computer. This would allow the computer to get smarter.

The computers would also recommend a fee that should be paid to each person involved in the care of the patient.

The second stage would allow the patient to actually input information into the system. This would be based on laboratory results received or from the patient's personal family history or their own devices. The medical computer could then make a diagnosis for treatments with the doctor's assistance. The patient could enter into the system things they think they have wrong and what pain they have, and the doctor can then ask the patient to help look for further analysis or give an adhocracy culture diagnosis and medication treatment and send it to the pharmacist for a prescription.

You will note that today, many people are using Google, and inputting pains they have, and getting back recommendations on what to do. This system will be much more accurate in a corporate culture database system. Doctors must use the system, but if they do not want to go to the second or future stages, they can stay with stage one of the Medical Computer. If some countries want to stay with just stage 1, it is their choice but recommended that all countries use all five stages but may take their time in going from one stage to another.

The third stage would allow for devices to be made that would scan the body and input information into a computer, and then diagnoses could be made and given to their doctor. You have seen some of these devices in the store today that allow a patient to take their own temperature, and blood pressure, as well as test blood samples themselves. A doctor or patient uses one of these devices that can be used to test something, but it has to be done by themselves to update their own patient's data in real time.

These future devices will allow us to do X-rays, test blood, and many other things which would allow you to detect cancer and treat other diseases yourself. This would allow us to uncover diseases at an early stage since it would be inexpensive to use, and everyone would have useful insight. Up-to-date data on old to new patients which would need to be supplied to a medical computer using with the persons actual treatment status or previous diagnosis therapies and post that based upon information from all institutions. There are also online psych websites that can reevaluate and access a pre-existing illness which can be done easily online to start new and reevaluate an older patient.

The fourth stage would allow for prescriptions or cures to be made automatically with doctor's approval. If a doctor wanted to override the Medical Computer, the doctor would have to justify why. This would allow the Medical Computer to get smarter. It is estimated that this will allow patients to communicate more with doctors, stop the escalating cost of medical treatment, and help them do it themselves. In all cases, money does not enter into methods of diagnosis or treatment because cost-cutting is part of the corporate culture system. Only the best method of curing a diagnosed illness is a consideration, and it is determined by the history of past cures that have worked for any illness.

The fifth stage would have the system diagnose based on patient input and direct the patient to the best service provider in their area and outside their area. The doctors will monitor the system occasionally to make sure it is operating correctly. This means that the best specialists and hospitals will get most of the business.

During the first phase, the patients or employees will use the output from the medical computer as a second opinion. If the medical computer is wrong in its recommendation, then the medical computer will be able to update itself with the reevaluation results of patients so it can get smarter when it makes the next recommendation.

This will help individual people because the output from the computer will not only recommend the best treatment for a person, but also where the best treatment can be done. When the computer is used worldwide, it will recognize when people in a specific area are coming down with the same illness. The Medical Computer can then recognize when a virus is just starting and make it known to everyone so action can be taken to keep the virus from spreading worldwide. Suppose the medical computer was operational when COVID started in China. In that case, it could have been stopped at that location.

The world needs the USA to put together a small group to start, finish, and test the Medical Computer and then sell it to other countries.

Other alternatives to healthcare can be reached through government intervention, such as more self-preventative healthcare. Right now, we buy stuff like this ourselves, such as cataracts or viruses, so we can already fix problems and find solutions that took years of discovery. One example is your eyes getting bad when you get old, which can be prevented. One adhocracy culture treatment you do yourself is cure cataracts with drops you buy at the store.

Since your eyes' lenses are not getting any benefits from blood, they get damaged proteins in the lenses. The eyes' lenses need a supplement of the eyedrop nutrients they are not getting from the body. The lenses get cloudier sometimes usually it goes away but sometimes it doesn't and cataracts develop, but even that cloudiness and eye problems can be reversed by taking a pill that corrects vision problems called oculotrophin PMG. The FDA didn't give a warning letter with it like they did with oclumed and immusist original. One of the ingredients they have is N-Acetyl-L-Carnosine, glutathione, and L-Taurine. If you want to prevent getting cloudy eyes or cataracts, you can buy something like OcluMed eye drops.

If you ever catch a virus or contagious disease from a sick person, and you don't usually get sick by yourself, like me. Once I caught the flu, they said it was the flu, but it was more like the coronavirus. It could have been a different type of flu that was similar to the coronavirus that occurred five months before the coronavirus was declared a pandemic. I was in the same room as the guy; he was coughing and exhaling all over the place where I was breathing, and I got something like the coronavirus. I couldn't inhale all the way; I couldn't stop coughing, and I had a slight fever. I tried brachial dilators so I could breathe, but that didn't work because there was a virus behind it. But then I tried some CitriCare, and usually I would only use ten drops of CitriCare about once a week, but because I was really sick, I used more CitriCare. I took about twenty to forty drops of CitriCare in a cup of water every day for about two weeks until it went away. If we had the Medical Computer, then I could look up what it would recommend and probably got the solution of CitriCare and prevented a call to the doctor or two weeks of pain.

In addition to the Medical Computer providing information to stop the spread of an unknown virus, we can also look to the Medical Computer to provide preventative nutritional and diet information on reversing metabolic syndrome, which we have to do ourselves right now ad hoc.

We need to help ourselves and it should done by using the new medical computer system. The Medical Computer, if it were available today, would be advising me to be on a very low-carb ketogenic diet, which would help your blood markers if they were checked, and the markers would be better than if you took the drugs they gave you. The way you're cutting carbs and sugar is by lowering glucose. You have better cholesterol, not the bad oxidized LDL, and your blood pressure is lower. With this diet, you use ketones for fuel instead of glucose, and your body makes ketones for fuel. By doing this, your body has less glucose available, and the body only gets 25% of its energy from glucose. It's very important that you have enough ketones, though with less glucose, since the other 75% of your energy comes from just ketones since you have no carbs in your keto diet. Just in case the ketones/glucose ratio is not right, I would definitely boost the ketones higher, as you know since glucose is already low. So I would take something to make more ketones, just in case yours are low and your body needs them. There is a supplement called beta-hydroxybutyrate (BHB), a chemical produced by the body. It provides energy when not enough carbohydrates or sugars have been eaten.

BHB can also be made in the lab and taken as a supplement. It helps the brain and nerves work better. It might also provide energy to muscles, improving exercise ability. You can buy this on Amazon; it's pretty cheap. You know your keto-friendly diet won't affect the energy your body needs from ketones by boosting them with a supplement to keep it running right or affecting your blood sugar potential by doing a keto diet. Shave off glucose by not eating more than 60 grams of carbohydrates daily and optimize the ketones with BHB. This is both healthcare systems the new one you do yourself, and pay for yourself, and the old one that's with insurance the old one that has limited potential and that institutions use. The old one has been used for a very long time in a way they think you have a very limited body potential. The new blood table system represents an undetermined potential or an infinite amount of our body's potential.

New Systems Blood Table

1/0.	1/0.	1/0.	1/0.	1/0.	1/0.	1/0.	1/0.	1/0.	1/0.	1/0.	1/0.	1/0.
1/0.	1/0.	1/0.	1/0.	1/0.	1/0.	1/0.	1/0.	1/0.	1/0.	1/0.	1/0.	1/0.
1/0.	1/0.	1/0.	1/0.	1/0.	1/0.	1/0.	1/0.	1/0.	1/0.	1/0.	1/0.	1/0.

1/0.	1/0.	1/0.	1/0.	1/0.	1/0.	1/0.	1/0.	1/0.	1/0.	1/0.	1/0.	1/0.
1/0.	1/0.	1/0.	1/0.	1/0.	1/0.	1/0.	1/0.	1/0.	1/0.	1/0.	1/0.	1/0.
1/0.	1/0.	1/0.	1/0.	1/0.	1/0.	1/0.	1/0.	1/0.	1/0.	1/0.	1/0.	1/0.
1/0.	1/0.	1/0.	1/0.	1/0.	1/0.	1/0.	1/0.	1/0.	1/0.	1/0.	1/0.	1/0.
1/0.	1/0.	1/0.	1/0.	1/0.	1/0.	1/0.	1/0.	1/0.	1/0.	1/0.	1/0.	1/0.
1/0.	1/0.	1/0.	1/0.	1/0.	1/0.	1/0.	1/0.	1/0.	1/0.	1/0.	1/0.	1/0.

Old Systems Blood Table

0/1.	0/1.	0/1.	0/1.	0/1.	0/1.	0/1.	0/1.	0/1.	0/1.	0/1.	0/1.	0/1.	0/1.
0/1.	0/1.	0/1.	0/1.	0/1.	0/1.	0/1.	0/1.	0/1.	0/1.	0/1.	0/1.	0/1.	0/1.
0/1.	0/1.	0/1.	0/1.	0/1.	0/1.	0/1.	0/1.	0/1.	0/1.	0/1.	0/1.	0/1.	0/1.
0/1.	0/1.	0/1.	0/1.	0/1.	0/1.	0/1.	0/1.	0/1.	0/1.	0/1.	0/1.	0/1.	0/1.
0/1.	0/1.	0/1.	0/1.	0/1.	0/1.	0/1.	0/1.	0/1.	0/1.	0/1.	0/1.	0/1.	0/1.
0/1.	0/1.	0/1.	0/1.	0/1.	0/1.	0/1.	0/1.	0/1.	0/1.	0/1.	0/1.	0/1.	0/1.
0/1.	0/1.	0/1.	0/1.	0/1.	0/1.	0/1.	0/1.	0/1.	0/1.	0/1.	0/1.	0/1.	0/1.
0/1.	0/1.	0/1.	0/1.	0/1.	0/1.	0/1.	0/1.	0/1.	0/1.	0/1.	0/1.	0/1.	0/1.
0/1.	0/1.	0/1.	0/1.	0/1.	0/1.	0/1.	0/1.	0/1.	0/1.	0/1.	0/1.	0/1.	0/1.

One time, while I was in the hospital, my psychiatrist told me my liver enzymes weren't right. Later, I didn't feel right, so I first tried to buy supplements. I got omega-3 and CoQ10, which helped my cardiovascular system, but my enzymes still needed to be fixed or replaced. I tried replacing my enzymes with proteolytic enzyme supplements, but that is expensive and probably doesn't work, and you still need to detox the toxins in the liver, which are preventing enzymes from forming in the liver. I would rather fix enzymes myself. I used Immusist and CitriCare; it works but that is too much oil that takes out the body's nutrients. You can't buy immusist anymore but you can buy their new product called immusist advance and you should use it if your worried about enzymes or for other health issues. They have good foods that help detox the liver including bone broth, cheese, tomatoes, coconut oil, and cayenne pepper and chili powder and walnuts, and more.

Everybody has heard of "green eggs and ham" and "the cat in the hat." Green eggs and ham together would be very high in omega-6.

Having a lot of meat and eggs with omega-6 fatty acids in them for breakfast and dinner would dangerously raise your omega-6 levels. A normal ratio of omega-6 to omega-3 should be close to 2/1. But if you ate both meals that had omega-6s in them, then you would have to take five fish oil pills every day or more to counteract the inflammatory problems caused by the omega-6s. What I do is switch to powders to stop that and still do the rest of the stuff. A powdered breakfast only has 18 grams of carbs and no omega 6. These powders you would need if you don't eat carbs, or eat paleo, Mediterranean, or enough vegetables. Fiber powder, green foods, collagen peptides, and spirulina are all good options. Collagen peptides have eight of the nine essential amino acids the body requires to make protein in the body. Spirulina powder is a blue-green algae that is a very potent cardiovascular and anti-inflammatory nutrient. Astronauts discovered that eating spirulina helped keep them from experiencing a cardiovascular collapse in space. So powders can be great for staying on a low-carb diet that's under 50g of carbs. Otherwise, if you don't want to take the powder option, do one meal a day or two meals a day made of whole food, and be sure you get the portions right to stay keto-friendly. Try to eat one or both meals within a six-hour window so you can still intermittently fast at night. A seventeen-hour intermittent fasting window works best to keep glucose within tolerance. You don't want to be in ketosis for long periods of time or very often. Therefore, if you eat enough whole foods with the right nutrients and stay under 60 grams of carbs a day, that works. When I was under thirty, I took more omega-3s and CoQ10, but when I was in my forties, I had insulin resistance T2D getting worse.

Then, when I got over fifty, things started to slide, and the insulin resistance T2D was getting way worse, and I was actually a real case of insulin-resistance type-2 diabetes. You can say in your living will that you have a terminal condition and that it's called metabolic syndrome, insulin-resistance type-2 diabetes, or syndrome X for that purpose. Metabolic reversal is a condition, but it's not a terminal condition. Metabolic syndrome is reversible. However, you can say in your living will that if it is a terminal condition, you fix yourself for that purpose. You can even give a twelve-year-old kid insulin resistance, type-2 diabetes, or metabolic syndrome. I did mostly all of the metabolic reversal stuff listed in this book mostly after I was fifty, but you might not need to do as many of these things until you are older. Be careful and worry about more of the things mentioned in this book as you get older and have to know more about your body. Think of it as a spiritual awakening. I don't think we have an infinite mind; it's the body that has infinite power. I wanted it to be easier than soup, so I found a new product called zeolite. There is a liposomal kind from Revel Health and many more zeolite brands from many other suppliers. They come in different-sized nanoparticles, some smaller-sized nanoparticles in liquids and powders. Some must be better than others. Detoxing with zeolite removes toxins and enzymes from the liver and body and can prevent cancer. This will patch up the enzymes for enzyme reproduction problems caused by toxins in the liver. Reconnecting the whole enzyme in the body would heal and make real enzymes. They know enzymes are not replicating properly in the liver because the liver gets toxins; this can be from just foods. This can affect how the enzyme structures are formed; for the enzymes to still work right, they must be formed correctly. However, this really isn't cancer; it's detoxifying the liver and making enzymes, and it's about metabolism and equilibrium. After cleansing your liver, you can now protect yourself by using a zeolite detox kit to get rid of toxins and make new enzymes.

Another way to detox the liver is to take L-Serin and glycine which are amino acids together to make glutathione which helps the heart and control blood pressure as well as detox the liver. Serin and glycine are two of my favorites because they help make glutathione and help control blood pressure and help moods are the most important supplements that are here compared to any other supplements mentioned.

There is a supplement called beta-hydroxybutyrate (BHB), which is a chemical that is made by the body. It provides energy when not enough carbohydrates or sugars have been eaten. These chemicals are normally made in your body in the liver, but as you get older, the body doesn't make enough of them.

One more important thing to know if you are on a very low-carb, high-fat diet: First off, the very low-carb ketogenic diet can increase insulin sensitivity and impart glucose tolerance. But if you do a very low-carb ketogenic diet in the long term, it can raise glucose intolerance and decrease insulin sensitivity. You might want to do one diet and then the other, and when you're doing the ketogenic fasting diet, you can also take beta-hydroxybutyrate to increase ketones and burn more energy from fat. Only take beta-hydroxybutyrate before meals, but intermittently and at intervals when you diet because BHB slows the secretion of insulin in the liver, which is what you need to lower glucose. BHB is better to take if you're doing the ketogenic diet rather than the regular diet because, on the ketogenic diet, you need to make more ketones to burn fat faster because you're burning 75% of your fat for energy. However, BHB is a tradeoff because you still need insulin to keep glucose down. Furthermore, BHB causes the liver to slow the production of insulin to make more ketones. You don't really want to take nearly as much sugar on the regular diet because you could raise the glucose levels from not having as much insulin. However, you could do a very low-carb ketogenic diet and take BHB, and then switch back to a regular diet with carbs and no BHB, and then do the ketogenic diet again later and take more BHB. There is a shopper's problem where somebody gets the wrong bottle, takes it, and gets cancer, so be sure to read your labels. The very low-carb ketogenic diet can increase insulin sensitivity in the short term, but it's a curve, so you should do it at intervals because a very low-carb, high-fat diet in the long term can decrease insulin sensitivity and raise glucose intolerance. Do the very low-carb ketogenic diet at intervals and take BHB to boost ketones and burn fat faster, but don't forget that it stops insulin secretion, so you would want to take a little more BHB on the ketogenic diet. In treating diabetes when you're on the regular diet or the ketogenic diet, you should supplement it with bitter melon, jiaogulan, hesperidin, and berberine. One other important thing you need to do is reoxygenate and dehydrogenate the blood a lot every day using alkaline water raising the pH. Add spirulina, green tea, and coffee to the alkaline water to prevent oxidative stress and low oxygenation of the blood. There is a deadly condition with blood called ischemia hyper-fusion where your blood has a low pH, low oxygenation, and low hydrogenation, and this blood then flows into organs and causes more tissue damage. Ischemia hyper-fusion occurs when your low-oxygenated blood goes back into tissues and causes further damage to tissues and organs that already have low blood oxygen and low ph. You should drink something immediately—alkaline water or anything—if you think this is happening.

As stated earlier in the book, when taking supplements and before consulting a doctor about drugs for treatment, make sure the doctor agrees that the supplements, ketogenic diet, and BHB, as well as the medicines you take, do not conflict. You can get dangerously low blood sugar, or hypoglycemia, if you combine treatments with drugs like metformin with supplements like these and the VLCKD. Be cautious when diagnosing the old corporate culture system and how the bureaucratic system is now. Right now, you can even get off drugs and buy your own supplements that deal with and treat schizophrenia and other illnesses yourself. I do not suggest you do this without your psychiatrist or doctors approval and supervision. However, there are therapies and drugs available from doctors, as well as supplements for diseases such as depression that you can take without ever being diagnosed, such as L-Serine, Glycine, and Citicoline. L-Serin makes your brain make more serotonin, which could work as well as a selective serotonin reuptake inhibitor that you would get from a doctor. Also, it depends on what the individual wants to do or what they can do for themselves. If you took both the supplement treatments mentioned above and the drugs for depression from regular medicine and cultures, you could get a dangerously high level of serotonin. I would recommend eating seaweed and drinking green tea with alkaline water to get enough nutritional benefits your doctor doesn't give you if that happens. I would also detox your gut and body with zeolite, so your body still makes your enzymes correctly and removes toxins from your liver.

The current medical system needs to be replaced with the system described in this book and *The Medical Project* book by Nicholas Licausi. We have talked to some people in government, and they have said that if a project like this came to them then they would agree to it. When all this is said and done, we will fix the medical system as described in this book and also in *The Medical Project* book before we run out of money using Medicare and Medicaid, and people will also find that the new corporate environment system is better. When the money runs out of Medicare, we'll just have the do-it-yourself system left. Also, the new system means doing some healthcare stuff yourself with the help of medical computers and also doctors using the medical computer. In four years, all there is going to be there is going to be enough money for social security, but we will need the medical system to change and add in the Medical Computer so we can still have enough money for Medicare and Medicaid. Also with the new medical system, we need to slim down the power of the FDA and should look at how supplements can be used rather than some drugs in curing or putting diseases in remission. Also, we need to talk about people with schizophrenia similar to the way we talk about people with any disease that goes into remission. It is important that if doctors and caregivers know that the previously diagnosed schizophrenic has a good recent history, was recently reevaluated, is taking all their medicines, and seem normal, then the person should be diagnosed as being in remission. Treatment of schizophrenia should be updated and talked about in a similar way to how you talk about another disease, even with tele psychiatry. Anybody that wants a helping hand can do an online psychiatric reevaluation, which is available now and would determine anyone's actual mental status. They would talk about their lives and be evaluated and diagnosed, if needed, with recommended therapies of counseling and medication. Usually, if you've been previously diagnosed and are in remission, they will say you have no symptoms of psychiatric disorders and give you a drug therapy you can do at home as a patient on a tele psychiatry website, which is faster and way better. Also by taking the supplements like Willard water or alkaline water and spirolina and hesperadin and reverse the underlying causes of cardiovascular disease, blood pressure, diabetes, and other problems mentioned in this book. But by having a normal blood pressure of 130/80 is not as important or as high of a risk, as someone who does not take any of these supplements and drink the water mentioned and who has high blood pressure. Also it is normal when you're running or doing high-intensity workouts or are under a lot of stress to have a higher blood pressure at least temporarily than 130/80. It's not normal to force your blood pressure to always be low and always remain in the normal or even high ranges. If it's high for a long time, you should get on a blood pressure drug to lower it together with supplements with blood pressure drugs and do both. By doing this prevents problems later like with kidneys and you prevent all the illnesses and diseases the best way humanly possible.

We enjoyed writing this book together. It was very hard to bring back memories where we both made mistakes. It was also bringing back nice memories that were great when the family was together. We loved being around each other. We were always laughing and having fun.

There are just two of us now since both ladies have passed on to heaven. They always had fun shopping and just being together. We are sure they are having fun together in heaven.

They are probably the ones that got us together and guided us in writing this book. Let's now hope we can get this Medical Computer built so we can make the lives of everyone a little better.

Listed below are all the supplements and medicines I take for blood pressure, heart, NRF2, diabetes, and anti-aging. As I said previous, make sure you check with you doctor to ensure these are okay for you.

- NAC N-Acetyl Cystene - blood pressure, cvd
- L-Serin, lower blood pressure w/ more glutathione, clean liver

- Glycine, helps lower blood pressure w/ more glutathione, clean liver
- L-Arginine, for Nitric Oxide precursor and blood pressure
- Jiaogulan-Gynostemma Pentaphyllum, for diabetes, cvd, ampk activation
- Berberis Aristata Root extract, for diabetes, Cvd, ampk
- Hespiradin, ampk, cvd, diabetes
- Bitter Mellon, simulates insuline in taking down sugar
- Omega 3, to prevent cvd by fixing the omega-3/omega-6 ratio
- Beta-Hydroxybutyrate (BHB), increases ketones to burn fat energy in ketosis
- Sulforaphane glucosinolate, nuclear factor eurythroid 2 activator, cvd
- Turmeric Curcumen, nrf2 activator for cardiovascular response
- Resveratrol helping the immune system
- Ginseng + Ginko biloba for Nitric oxide distribution, blood
- Niagen, nicotinamide riboside chloride, to make NAD+ anti aging activating sirtuins
- NMN, Nicotinamide mononucleotide, to make NAD + anti-aging activating sirtuins
- Apigenin, to prevent senescent cells from causing inflammation, cvd
- Vitamin K2 to help calcium absorbtion
- CoQ10, heart health
- Vitamin B-Complex all B vitamins restores healing nerves
- Plant sterols - Beta Sitosterol helps shrink prostate
- Magnesium L-Threonate help calms the brain
- Essential Amino Acids give body all nine it needs to make proteins
- Brown seaweed – fucoidan, decrease amount of senescent cells by apoptosis
- Nettles and green tea cleans and help kidneys function at higher capacity

- Natural liquid Zeolite – everyday gut and body detox, helps detox liver for enzymes
- Foods raw organic fiber for insulin-resistance type-2 diabetes and help digestion
- Foods collagen peptides, and nine essential amino acids, for all necessary protein prod
- Foods greens blend, amazing grass, era fiber blend, digestive enzymes pre-, pro-biotic, speed up metabolic equilibrium
- Foods, coffee, .5 lb ground meat a day w/tomato powder, high fat low carb, ketovore
- Suppl: Dulse seaweed to replenish nutrients the body need k2, sea veg aminos.
- Suppl: Organic spirolina to help cardiovascular system repair itself from oxidative dis.
- Suppl: Willard water with high ph alkaline water to remineralize and clean out guts rehydrogenate, oxygenate

Living Wills for Following the Patient's Wishes. If a competent patient refuses care, either directly or through a living will or surrogate, the physician is bound to respect those wishes. This does not apply to euthanasia or living wills that violate state law.